Who is Gail Riplinger?

A Warning for God's Sheep

By Aletheia O'Brien

Who Is Gail Riplinger? A Warning for God's Sheep

© July, 2010
Aletheia O'Brien

All rights reserved. No part of this publication may be reproduced, stored in a retrieval system, or transmitted in any form or by any means (electronic, mechanical, photocopying, recording, or otherwise), except in the case of brief quotations in articles and reviews where the context is maintained.

Unless otherwise stated, scripture is from the King James Bible

Published by the Dean Burgon Society
August, 2010

ISBN 978-1-56848-072-5

Address all inquiries to:

Dean Burgon Society
P. O. Box 354
Collingswood, NJ 08108
USA

Phone: 865-854-4452
Orders: 1-800-John 10:9
FAX: 865-854-2464
BFT #3477
E-mail: DBS@DeanBurgonSociety.org
Website: www.DeanBurgonSociety.org

The Dean Burgon Society (DBS) publishes materials and books that it believes will be helpful to individuals. Although the DBS may not necessarily endorse everything in a work, if the writing presents information that is critical to a debate, then the text is published.

Dedicated to my one and only husband and to my son, the most precious of earthly treasures

"Every good gift and every perfect gift is from above, and cometh down from the Father of lights, with whom is no variableness, neither shadow of turning."
- James 1:17

"But thanks be to God, which giveth us the victory through our Lord Jesus Christ."
- 1 Corinthians 15:57

Who is Gail Riplinger?
Part One

"Truth is independent of who presents it."
    – Gail Riplinger (1994),
    Which Bible is God's Word?, p. 5.

"Behold, thou desirest truth in the inward parts."
    – Psalm 51:6

Context is Everything

A recurring theme in Gail Riplinger's interviews and church lectures is her comparison of herself to certain righteous women of the Bible such as Jael, Deborah, the wise woman of 2 Samuel, and Mary Magdalene. Such comparisons are intended to explain why she, a woman, is justified in teaching the church about the Bible and from church pulpits where men are present in the congregation. In several church lectures, filmed in the mid 1990s, Mrs. Riplinger explained the following:

    1.) The second question I receive most often is the lady question. You know, **what's a lady doing up there?** ... And, so, **I'll answer that** very, very quickly ... Those of you who know the Bible ... know that **it's merely a *type*,** ok? Let me go through a couple verses. If you have a pencil, you can write these down. But when you start **in Judges chapter 4 and 5, it said: "Every man did that which was right in his own eyes,"** ok? ... [I]mmediately after that happens you have Deborah and Jael showing up, and it says: "The Lord shall sell Sisera into the hand of a woman," ok? Because "every man did that which was right in his own eyes."** Ok, in Judges chapter 9, verse 53, we have an incident of Abimelech, and you know Abimelech was the usurper. ... So, when we have the usurper showing up, as we have the new Bible versions today usurping the voice of Almighty God. The way God killed Abimelech was to have a woman in a tower—and the tower obviously represents the King James Bible—or the word of God—you know, the Hebrew or Greek, or whatever—but represents the word of God.

You have a woman in a tower, and she threw a millstone on his head and **she killed him**. And immediately Abimelech said to his servant, ah, quote, 'Slay me, that men say not of me, a woman slew him,' ok? Now, Abimelech was willing to die 'that men say not of me'—he was worried about what people say, ok? And as long as someone's worried about what people say, ah, [pause]. You know, God had a woman do it because the ultimate insult to an egotistical Greek professor would be a disabled home economist, ok?

Number three, 2 Samuel 20:16—now, **I'm just showing you some of the *types* in the Bible, so you'll understand.** Ah, **Joab, ah, went to what was called—so-called—the wise woman**, and she went to all the people in her wisdom, it said. ... she went to all the people in her wisdom and Joab said to her, ah—or she said, 'Hear the words of thy [sic] handmaiden.' He said, 'I do hear.' Ok, so **we have *that* typology there.** ... And the verse that the Lord gave me is, ah, Mary Magdalene going to the, ah, the tomb ... and, ah, **the men were afraid, ah, the men were looking for Prozac** [laughs], wherever they could find, and hiding away [laughs] ...

2.) The Old Testament says that Sisera oppressed Israel for 20 years. And then God brought Jael, who stayed in her tent ... and she put the tent peg through his head, ok? And that was the end of him, because it was a head problem, you know. Pride, all right? ... **[T]he Lord showed me** the same story with Abimelech. ... And [God] said, "This is why we're doing this, Gail. You're gonna do this." [Laughs] I said, "Oh, swell," you know? And there was the, um, Sheba—Sheba's head—and the, and the wise woman with Joab. So, God seems to have—**He doesn't use women to teach**, He doesn't use women to preach. **He just uses women to kill people** [laughs]**, ok?** ... This is my ammunition pack, here. **This is my sword and we'll take a few heads off if we have to** [laughs].[1] [Emphasis added]

Contrary to what Gail Riplinger taught these church congregations, neither Judges 4 nor 5 say: "Every man did that which was right in his own eyes." Those words occur *only* in Judges 17:6 and 21:25, long after Sisera lay dead with the tent peg in his temple, Abimelech was run through, and Sheba was beheaded. They do not have anything to do with the times of Deborah, Jael, Sisera, Sheba, or Joab. The accounts of Deborah and Jael subduing an enemy

---

[1] The first quote is from a video sent to me on a DVD by a King James Only believer. It had no title on it other than "NKJV" handwritten on the label. In it, the name of the church where she was speaking is not identified. In this video, Riplinger lectures to a full congregation, using an overhead projector, with two men in suits sitting behind her. The second quote is from the "Riplinger Lecture Series," titled Research Update, Q & A, King James Bible Perfection or NIV, NKJV, NASV, Perversions (sold by Riplinger), filmed at Temple Baptist Church, Knoxville, TN, 1996. The two pictures are still frames from the video, showing Riplinger teaching in the pulpit of Temple Baptist Church, Knoxville, TN.

take place in Judges 4. Therefore, Deborah and Jael did not "immediately show up" after "Every man did that which was right in his own eyes," since the historical events of Judges 4 chronologically *precede* those of Judges 17 and 21. Deborah and Jael are not mentioned again in scripture after the events of Judges 5. Riplinger has combined two separate chronological events together as one, making the latter precede the earlier. This is just one example of how she takes Scripture out of its correct context in her books and lectures.

Whenever we read the word of God, *context is key*. The context of Judges 17:6 is: "Every man did that which was right in his own eyes" *because* "in those days *there was no king* in Israel." Therefore, as chapter 17 explains, a disobedient man named Micah did what was right in his own eyes when he made a pagan shrine and consecrated one of his sons as a priest. This historical account of an era in Israel's existence (following Judges 17:6) says nothing about women taking the authority where men refuse to act. If we are not going to read (or teach) scripture in the context in which God gave it, we dangerously alter (change) God's word. We must also be careful to accept only the teaching of those who teach God's word *in context*.

Riplinger also incorrectly made the woman in the tower the person who *killed* Abimelech, telling her audience: "she threw a millstone on his head and **she killed him**." She then had Abimelech speaking to his armor-bearer immediately after she said the woman "killed him." Riplinger was confused about the story, yet presented it as if she knew what she was talking about, even telling her audience that the Lord "showed" her these things. How could God show her things that never occurred in the sequence in which she places them? She left off the end of Judges 9:54, where it says his armor-bearer, a *man*, actually *killed* Abimelech, at Abimelech's request: "And **his young man thrust him through**, and [then] *he died*." Yes, Abimilech might have eventually died of complications from the head wound the woman gave him but it was the armor bearer's sword that immediately *ended* Abimelech's life, in this context.

Yet again, Riplinger incorrectly taught scripture in 2 Samuel 20:16. Joab did not *"go to* the wise woman"; she *came seeking him*. And she was not *"the* wise woman" but *"a* wise woman," as KJV scripture correctly points out (2 Samuel 20:16), meaning she was probably not the *only* wise woman who lived in the city of Abel but that she was called *wise* because she offered to help Joab find Sheba. The woman humbly appealed to Joab, telling him she was among the faithful of Israel (2 Samuel 120:19). In doing so, she asked Joab not to destroy her city. Joab explained that destroying the city was not his wish but that it would be necessary if the people did not deliver Sheba to him. Then the woman said Sheba's head would be cast over the city's wall and thus delivered to Joab. The woman accomplished this by informing the people that Joab would destroy their city unless Sheba was delivered to him. The people, not wanting their city to be destroyed, promptly found Sheba, cut off his head, and threw it out to Joab. Riplinger omitted the true context of the story by isolating verse 16 out of context from the rest of the passage, thus telling the story *her* way. So, what exactly was the "typology" Riplinger was attempting to give her audience? That she is a "wise woman" sent to "cut off" the heads of Bible scholars, when she cannot exegete scripture correctly? Was she implying that she is the "handmaiden" of God sent to the church, justified in teaching men? How do the events of the wise woman of Abel allow for *that*? Riplinger continued in these lectures to exegete scripture passages before the congregations and *teach* on such biblical subjects as "the blood" and its meaning in the Bible, etc. Why did the pastors of these churches allow her to teach scripture, and out of context? No one can honestly deny that she was teaching in the church assembly, something forbidden in scripture.

When a person teaches about the people and events of Bible history, it is imperative that the information be correct. Riplinger's errors disqualify her as a teacher; her gender disqualifies her as teacher of men. She even admitted (she knows) that God does *not* use (allow) women to teach and preach. Yet, what she is doing in these church lectures is teaching. The main problem with this is she is teaching in the church meeting where men are present, placing them under her teaching authority. She even told the congregation to write down the verses she was going to give them, as she taught them incorrectly why she believe she is a "type."

Why didn't at least one of the men present in the congregation defend the context of the word of God by speaking up to correct her? She falsely represented the historical period and details of Deborah, Jael, and the wise woman of Abel, to justify her teaching in churches where a man, such as *her husband*, should be instead. Were the men sitting in the congregation so unfamiliar with the scripture that they could not spot such simple errors and correct her as she taught the Bible out of context? Were they afraid to speak up? If Riplinger's actions were an object lesson showing men *not* taking the leadership that God has laid on them, perhaps many of the pastors who allowed her to teach from their pulpits might realize their part in the problem.

Where was Gail's husband? She was usurping authority over men while making it appear as if that is what Jael and Deborah did. The guidelines for the church are clear, as scripture states:

> But I suffer not a woman **to teach**, nor to **usurp authority over the man**, but to be in silence (1 Timothy 2:12).

Even if "the man" refers only to the woman's *husband*, it only makes sense that if she is not allowed to teach or usurp authority over her husband then *she is also not permitted to teach or usurp authority over the men in the local church assembly*. However, while Paul could have said "husband" in this edict, he did not. Paul was not giving marital advice only but instruction concerning authority in church organization. Paul's main point is that in Christ it is the man who is in charge, whether in the home or in the church assembly, not the woman. In his epistles to Timothy, Paul was instructing the young pastor about *proper conduct* and *order* when Christians comes together in the church meeting (assembly; corporate worship). It was Timothy's responsibility to know these things as an overseer. God is not the author of confusion and His word is quite clear. He is not going to forbid a woman from teaching or taking authority over her husband but then allow her to do so over other men (and other women's husbands) while *in* the church assembly. Men are the assigned authority in teaching and in keeping order, both at home and when the church body comes together. Church assembly, in many ways, mirrors the home. Riplinger's husband should have been the one lecturing and teaching, yet he has *never* taken that role. Why does Mr. Riplinger allow his wife to disregard scripture? Some of Mrs. Riplinger's lectures have even included question-and-answer sessions, where men—some of them pastors—have asked her questions about the Bible. Perhaps pastors who have to ask a woman questions about the Bible do not understand the woman's proper role in the church?[2] 1 Corinthians 14:34 backs up 1 Timothy 2:12 concerning "the woman" and church order, when it comes to the congregation. It is truly sad that some pastors are ignorant in this area of scriptural command or choose to overlook it. We have a weak church today because God's word is ignored, perhaps for convenience' sake.

Take note of how subtly Riplinger denigrated the men of the Bible in her erroneous comparison of herself with Mary Magdalene, saying such ludicrous things as "the *men* were looking for Prozac." You know, the snide, sexist women's libber bias: "Men are stupid, are usually good for nothing, and rarely get their act together (without sex or drugs); women are smarter and most often get it right." The men in the congregation did not pick up on that? They laughed as if they did not realize the joke was on them and not in a flattering way. King

---

[2] Some of these pastors include those of Temple Baptist Church, Knoxville, TN, and Berean Baptist Church, Winston-Salem, NC. A pastor's conference where pastors asked her questions is titled *Riplinger Testimony, Question & Answer*. The 2009 Annual Bus Convention at Clays Mill Road Baptist Church, Lexington, KY, included a question and answer session where men asked her questions about the Bible rather than their pastor (available from Clays Mill Road Baptist Church in audio format only). Riplinger's 2009 Bus Convention sessions can be listened to online at http://www.wpipbereanradio.org/truthevangelism.html.

James Only Bible believers especially should not allow her get away with that one, especially since "Prozac" is mentioned *nowhere* in the Bible and her taking license with it is completely unfunny and inappropriate. It is highly doubtful that Mary Magdalene would have made such an irreverent comment. Riplinger's remark was a subtle add-on to the scripture.

Contradictorily, *some* people who voice no concern over Gail Riplinger teaching the Bible in church pulpits happen to also agree with vociferous KJO preacher Phil Kidd who has made it clear that he is against women teaching in church in place of men.[3] It cannot be denied that she was indeed teaching in the church assembly where men were present.

Did Jael and Deborah Raise a False Report?

"Awake, awake, Deborah: awake, awake, utter a song…" –Judges 5:12

"Blessed above women shall Jael the wife of Heber the Kenite be…" –Judges 5:24

One of the most startling findings during my collation of *New Age Bible Versions* alongside the sources Riplinger used was that of repeated *falsehood*. There are so many misquotations and facts misrepresented within that the typos are insignificant. At first, I thought that perhaps she had accidentally misquoted her sources, then I checked them for myself. I discovered in chapter after chapter that the misquotations were rampant and clearly taken out of context. It was obvious they are not accidental. I found that a few people with whom

---

[3] Phil Kidd, evangelist and KJVO proponent, "Hey Lady Shut Up!" It can be read at http://www.jesus-is-savior.com/Evils%20in%20America/Feminism/shut_up.htm. The owner of Jesus-is-Savior.com is both pro-Riplinger and pro-Kidd, even though the two's theological practices oppose one another and make for a confusing theology combination. Is God the author of such confusion?

she shares an accord, such as Texe Marrs,[4] she quotes correctly, most of the time. This indicates she is able to quote people correctly when it benefits her cause.

If Jael and Deborah were asked today to assess the problems in Gail Riplinger's book, their wise counsel would certainly be to obey scripture, reject falsehood, and seek the truth. They would most likely agree wholeheartedly with the Bereans (who verified everything) and call on Gail Riplinger to recant her dishonesty.

How Many Husbands Did Jael and Deborah Have?

Riplinger's analogy and misapplication of scripture not only present a false right to take authority over men but, in comparing herself to these Godly women whose noble legacies have been eternally preserved in God's word, she left out a crucial detail. Scripture shows that each woman was the wife of *one* living husband (Judges 4:17, 12, and 5:24; Judges 4:4). They were faithful women who obeyed the Law of God, which clearly forbids divorce.[5]

Divorces Outside Scripture

Gail Riplinger has had two unscriptural divorces, both while a professing Christian (as her testimony indicates), and then she lied to cover them up when they were discovered. Neither of her first two husbands petitioned for the divorces; Gail did. Neither husband had

---

[4] In *New Age Bible Versions*, Riplinger refers frequently to the books *Dark Secrets of the New Age* and *Mystery Mark of the New Age*, both by Texe Marrs. In most cases, she quotes his work in context.

[5] While due to the hardness of hearts, Moses inserted into the Mosaic Law an allowance for divorce; yet, God has never accepted divorce, as Jesus explained (Matthew 19:3-11). From the beginning, God's way is right and eternally higher than man's.

committed marital unfaithfulness.[6] In the lectures quoted from above, she withheld the important information of her divorces from her audiences as she likened herself to these law-abiding women and claimed a false right to teach in church pulpits, despite 1 Corinthians 14:34. During the 1990s, as Riplinger visited various churches to teach on the King James Bible, she was an unlawfully divorced woman with two husbands living. Pastors who hold strong scriptural convictions concerning divorce and remarriage were not allowed to know about this before inviting her to speak to their congregations.

Interestingly, 19th-century occult leader Madame Helena Petrovna Blavatsky (H.P.B.), one of the New Age/occult sources most often cited by Riplinger in her argument against Modern English Versions, was herself divorced twice. It is highly likely that Riplinger, who has claimed she read all sorts of New Age material when she was in the New Age movement, studied Blavatsky's writings. Riplinger's detailed knowledge of Blavatsky's books, cited in *New Age Bible Versions*, seems to further indicate this.

Since the moral character of people who hold a position of teaching authority in the body of Christ is of high importance, the matter of Gail Riplinger's divorces, her covering them and then her lying about them needs to be addressed. The details in this booklet are the result of four years of in-depth research on the part of my husband and myself. We have studied her teachings and found many errors, and we have looked at the person doing the teaching. Because defending truth is of utmost importance, we must go into detail to address this situation. We are addressing "who is Gail Riplinger?" because a person's message is only as good as the messenger where the church is concerned. God says: "Be not deceived: evil communications corrupt good manners." Let us all take it to heart.

---

[6] In neither petition for divorce did Gail state "marital" or "sexual" unfaithfulness by her husbands as a reason for her wanting either divorce, even though if they had been unfaithful she could have, per the State of Ohio's allowances. Neither divorce record indicates any unfaithfulness. The reasons she gave were among those offered by the secular State of Ohio and are not allowed by scripture.

God Holds Character, the Sanctity of Marriage, and Honesty in Unwavering High Esteem

"...Provide things honest in the sight of all men." –Romans 12:17

"Providing for honest things, not only in the sight of the Lord, but also in the sight of men." –2 Corinthians 8:21

Someone has said, "But Mrs. Riplinger's divorces happened before she became a Christian, didn't they? So, they don't matter." That would be true *if* that were the case. But it isn't. In early 2007, we launched an intensive background investigation on Mrs. Riplinger and discovered the unscriptural nature of her divorces. In early 2008, after hearing that Mrs. Riplinger had told Dr. and Mrs. D.A. Waite that she had never been married to any man other than her current husband, Michael, we mailed copies of her marriage and divorce documents to them. Because she lied about them to the Waites, and to the Church at large, we made her divorce and marriage documents available on the Internet, so that those concerned could see the truth for themselves. Since she is a public teacher (having been invited to speak in many Independent Fundamental Baptist churches, and since her teaching is public record), she is a public figure who has influenced many people who have purchased her books and other materials—and who might have otherwise chosen not to if they had known the truth.

Therefore, the public has the right to know about this serious, holistic moral issue.

Even if her divorces were within proper scriptural guidelines (which they are not), it still would not give her license to lie about them. If she believes herself without guilt for obtaining the divorces, then why did she keep them secret and lie about them when they were discovered? After verifying her divorce documents for himself, Dr. D.A. Waite confronted Gail privately by phone during the summer of 2009, giving her the chance to explain why she had lied, which she declined. Dr. Waite went public with her denial and the divorce documents at his July 2009 Bible conference. People who trusted her for over a decade became concerned that she had lied about something as serious as divorce. Soon afterward, most likely realizing that the divorces were undeniable, Riplinger formed a story seemingly intended to pacify her following and make her *appear* innocent in obtaining the divorces. In a letter purported to be from her current pastor (Dewayne Sands of Believer's Baptist Church), Gail's daughter, Bryn Riplinger Shutt, was quoted explaining on behalf of her mother:

> Although [the events of her childhood and her divorces] were all monumentally heartbreaking to her, **she says that without them she may not have received Christ** [or recognized] her lost condition ... [Emphasis added] [7]

The words (which also appeared in a tribute to her parents' Silver Anniversary, which she wrote for the September 2009 issue of Mickey Carter's *Landmark Anchor*) give the appearance that Gail was not

---

[7] Bryn Riplinger Shutt is quoted in a letter reported by HACAlumni.com to be written by Gail Riplinger's Pastor, Dewayne Sands, of Believer's Baptist Church of Ararat, VA. The letter was placed on the Hyles Anderson Alumni web site (HACAlumni.com) in August 2009 as a rebuttal to Pastor Jack Schaap of First Baptist Church of Hammond and Hyles-Anderson College, Hammond, IN, after he had addressed the unscriptural nature of Gail Riplinger's divorces at his King James Bible Summit 2009. There is no doubt that the quoted words are those of Bryn Riplinger Shutt, since she included them, verbatim, in a tribute she wrote for her parents' silver wedding anniversary, included in the September 2009 issue of the *Landmark Anchor*, published by Landmark Baptist Church of Haines City, Florida (copy on file).

saved until *after* the time of the divorces and that the divorces helped her realize her need for the Lord. However, Riplinger's own words from the past contradict this story and point to yet more lies. According to Gail's own *public* testimony, given by her in several places during the 1990s, she was saved *before* the time of her divorces:

> I received the Lord Jesus Christ as my Savior when **I was 26 years old**... [8]

> It's been some **26 years** and he saved my wicked soul... [9]

> I was saved [at Kent State University] as a graduate student...I had a burden for the young ladies and I knew if someone didn't get a hold of these young ladies, you know, who knows where they'd go? Probably where I went between the ages of 16 and **26 years old by the time I'd gotten saved**. [10]

> I was a Catholic for **the first 26 years** of my life. [11]

---

[8] Riplinger stated this as part of her testimony during a two-hour lecture taped at Berean Baptist Church (4135 Thomasville Road, Winston-Salem, NC 27107) on Sunday morning, May 19, 1996. Sold on DVD by Mrs. Riplinger as Riplinger Lecture Series, *Overview: Sword Slays the Dragon, King James Bible Perfection or NIV, NKJV, NASV Perversion*, A.V. Publications, Corp., P.O. Box 280, Ararat, VA 24053. It can be viewed online at http://www.archive.org/details/Over_View_Riplinger.

[9] Ibid. When Riplinger gave this lecture she was about 52 years old. When the "some 26 years" is subtracted from 52, her age at the time of salvation is 26, the same age given by her in other places.

[10] Gail stated this as part of her testimony during a lecture taped at Temple Baptist Church (2100 W. Woodrow Drive, Knoxville, TN) in 1996. Sold by Mrs. Riplinger as *Riplinger Lecture Series: Research Update Q & A, Sword Slays the Dragon, King James Bible Perfection or NIV, NKJV, NASV Perversion*, A.V. Publications, Corp., P.O. Box 280, Ararat, VA 24053. It can be viewed online at http://www.archive.org/details/Questions_and_Answers_Riplinger.

[11] Ibid. Riplinger has said in several places that she was raised in a Catholic home by a Catholic mother. She was born in a Catholic hospital (Our Lady of Mt. Carmel of Columbus, OH) and lived in her Catholic grandparents' home

> I was raised as a Roman Catholic. ... And when I was saved [at 26] I left the Roman Catholic Church. [12]

> When I was **in my late 20s** I received the Lord Jesus as my Savior ... [13]

Gail Riplinger was born Gail Anne Ludwig in late 1947.[14] She turned 26 in 1973. She filed for the first divorce and a legal separation on October 17, 1974,[15] just days after her 27th birthday. The divorce became final on February 10, 1975.[16] She was 36 when she filed for her second, and most controversial, divorce,[17] which became final on

---

as a child. Obituaries for her grandparents indicate they were Catholic. She was married to her first husband in a Catholic church. When she says she was a Catholic for the first 26 years of her life, she means from birth. She states she left the Catholic Church upon salvation, at the age of 26.

[12] *Transparent Translations*, video, recorded at a Prophecy Club conference, filmed at a Kansas City TV station in the mid 1990s and broadcast over television and radio.

[13] *Nite Line features New Age Bible Versions*, (VHS) an interview with Gail Riplinger, c. 1995, Dove Broadcasting, Inc., P.O. Box 1616, Greenville, SC 29602. Apparently, Riplinger considers the age of 26 to be one's late 20s.

[14] Birth certificate of Gail Anne Ludwig. Born October 1947, in Columbus, OH, to Wilson B. and Helen G. (Frech) Ludwig. On file with the Office of Vital Records, Columbus, OH. In her interview with Mrs. Yvonne Waite, Riplinger states she was born in Columbus, Ohio, and reared in Niles, Ohio.

[15] *Gail Anne Latessa v. Terry Latessa*, case no. 74-DR-1543, February 10, 1975. On file at Mahoning County Court, 120 Market St., 2nd Floor, Youngstown, OH 44503.
www.mahoningcountyoh.gov/MahoningWeb/Department+and+Agencies/Department/Probate+Court/

[16] Ibid.

[17] *Gail Anne Kaleda v. Frank A. Kaleda*, case no. 84-CV0652, August 6, 1984. On file at Portage County Common Pleas, Clerk of Courts, P.O. Box 1035, Ravenna, OH 44266.
http://www.co.portage.oh.us/clerkofcourts.htm
http://www.portageco.com/misc_countyrecords.htm

August 6, 1984.[18] According to her testimony throughout the 1990s, she appeared quite certain of her age when she "left the Roman Catholic Church" and "became saved," both being monumental events in a person's life.

Moral purity should be an indisputable priority for Christians, as commanded by God. Lying about sin, to cover it up, is an abomination to God. When someone who is esteemed in the body of Christ—whether they are a pastor, leader, teacher, or author—is found guilty of willful sin, it must be addressed because the person is involved on a deep, personal level with the body of Christ. Even the Apostle Paul spoke of keeping himself in line lest he become disqualified. When the practice of sin is allowed to reign unchecked, the church ends up with the likes of Ted Haggard, Benny Hinn, Jim Baker, Peter Popoff, Paula White, Robert Tilton, Rick Warren and his New Age comrades Leonard Sweet, Rob Bell, etc., and the list goes on.

As of the printing of this exposé, Gail Riplinger has not yet personally acknowledged the disobedient nature of her divorces and her having lied about them. She seems content to allow her daughter—who was not there and who, therefore, knows nothing other than what her mother tells her—to speak on behalf of her divorces. Why is Gail hiding from the issue? Why does she not just acknowledge that the nature of her divorces and her hiding them from her following was wrong? Those church leaders that continue to ignore the elephant in the room, and who continue to invite Riplinger to speak to their congregations as if she holds no responsibility for her actions, are on many levels in direct disobedience to the word of God (Romans 1:32).

Covering Tracks? Saving Face? Protecting Book Sales?

"He that covereth his sins shall not prosper…"   –Proverbs 28:13a

---

[18] Ibid.

Willful Deception

By now, some might be asking: *But why would Mrs. Riplinger want to change or cover the facts?* First, there's the protection of her book sales (since 1993), a large source of income. At the time that the divorces became undeniable fact,[19] Mrs. Riplinger's sixth book, *Hazardous Materials*, had just left the printing press and was being marketed throughout the King James Bible world.

Second, there is the problem of all those pastors who trusted her, who now know the truth. They believed she was being honest with them about herself, when during the 1990s she gained their trust and they allowed her to teach doctrine to their congregations, from their church pulpits.[20] She portrayed herself as someone she was not. Some

---

[19] Dr. D.A. Waite addressed Riplinger's divorces publicly at his Bible Conference in July 2009 because he discovered that she had lied to him and Mrs. Waite when they'd phoned her in late 2007 to ask if the "rumors" that were circulating were true. At that time, Riplinger told them that she had never been married to any man other than her current husband. The Waites obtained certified court copies of Riplinger's marriage and divorce records and spoke to close acquaintances of the second husband, discovering that Riplinger had indeed been divorced twice in the past. This, among other things, prompted Mrs. Waite to write a private letter to Riplinger and address her concerns that Gail had lied to her and Dr. Waite. The Waites went public at the conference and made Mrs. Waite's letter public at http://www.bftbc.org/.PDF/BFT/UPDATE/ATTACHMENTS/RiplingerAnswer.098.pdf and also in their Bible for Today August 2009 newsletter: http://www.bftbc.org/.PDF/BFT/UPDATE/BFTUPDAT.098.pdf?utm_source=MailingList&utm_medium=email&utm_campaign=BFT+UPDATE+August+2009.

[20] Several of the videos already mentioned above show Riplinger teaching in churches where men are present in the congregations, despite 1 Timothy 2:11-14 where Paul instructed the young pastor on the proper order of God's church when in assembly. Some argue that this passage only pertains to women being subject to their husbands when at home. However, if it is the husband that is to teach the wife and not the wife that is to teach the husband then a woman would also not be permitted to teach other men at church. It only makes sense that this passage pertains to women both at home and at church, not just one or the other. 1 Corinthians 14:34-35 commands "Let your women keep silence in the **churches**: for it is not permitted unto them to

of these pastors—many of whom adhere to the clear scriptural rules regarding divorce and remarriage in the Scripture—could end up feeling betrayed by Riplinger's lack of moral forthrightness. They believed they could trust her. If Scripture lays out a set of rules for men who want to be pastors, deacons, elders, and teachers, then anyone (man or woman) who teaches doctrine (of any kind) in the church should also be held to biblical moral standards and seek to lead a life in obedience to God's word. Those pastors should have obeyed the rule in 1 Corinthians 14:34 concerning women speaking to the church when in assembly. Even if Riplinger wasn't teaching in those pulpits, the integrity of her life would still be an issue because she has been elevated as a core leader in the King James Bible world. If a man or woman does not have their life in proper order, they are in no capacity to teach any doctrine to the body of Christ. Christians are "living epistles" and the very act of what they do is who they are, and that matters for good or for bad in the body of Christ. The Apostle Paul stated, "But I keep under [discipline] my body, and bring it into subjection: lest that by any means, when I have preached to others, I myself should be a castaway [disqualified] (1 Corinthians 9:27)." This policy should be important to all. God's moral rules are for everyone. And it is the responsibility of pastors, as shepherds, to see that anyone they allow to occupy their pulpit is within the proper guidelines of Scripture, as well as in proper standing with God's word in their personal life. It is Riplinger's responsibility to acknowledge she was wrong.

---

speak…" The word *churches* is plural and is not just pertaining to the women of the Corinthian church. God has made men the authority and leaders in the Body of Christ, as 1 Timothy 2:13-14 and 1 Corinthians 11:3 indicate, both in the home and in the church assembly. This would also be the rule for pastors to not allow a woman to *teach* doctrine of any kind that concerns the word of God, as well as any other kind of doctrine, where men are present in the church assembly. God does not have one set of rules for Christian behavior outside the church assembly and another set for within it. God is a God of order and He changes not (Malachi 3:6, Hebrews 13:8).

The person who lies to cover the truth most often does so because he or she knows their behavior is wrong and that others will know the same if they find out about it. Jesus said:

> And this is the condemnation, that light is come into the world, and men loved darkness rather than light, **because their deeds were evil**. For every one that doeth evil hateth the light, **neither cometh to the light, lest his deeds should be reproved**. But he that doeth truth cometh to the light, that his deeds may be made manifest, that they are wrought in God....[H]e that walketh in darkness knoweth not whither he goeth. (John 3:19-21, 12:35b).

Darkness hides evil deeds; light exposes them. Truth is the obvious opposite of lying. A truly repentant attitude in a liar will outwardly show a change of heart concerning lying. The woman at the well knew she was wrong but had no problem admitting her multiple husbands. The difference between the woman at the well and Gail Riplinger is that the woman at the well humbly acknowledged her wrong. Her heart was turned toward repentance, not lies.

Lying Early On to the Church About Her Marital Status

In the 1990s, instead of sharing her divorces when talking about those parts of her life, Gail Riplinger was concealing them with lies even then, lying to the people who had put their trust in her, by fabricating a false story about herself. When she lectured to a group of pastors at the Gospel Light Baptist Church of Walkertown, NC, in the late 1990s,[21] she said:

---

[21] This lecture is sold by Riplinger's A.V. Publications, Corp., as part of the Riplinger Lecture Series: *Detailed Update: King James Bible Perfection, New Version Perversion* (Q & A with Pastors), recorded at Gospel Light Baptist Church, 890 Walkertown-Guthrie Rd., Walkertown, NC. Riplinger occasionally changes the titles of her lectures.

> **I was a professor at Kent State University.** Now, I don't want you to think I'm a woman's lib person or anything, cuz I don't believe—I believe women should be keepers at home. But **I wasn't married** ...

And to the congregation of Temple Baptist Church, Knoxville, TN:

> **I was a professor at Kent State University** for ten years and, um, I didn't have any children of my own, and I don't— I'm not women's lib, so I believe women should be keepers at home as best they can. But, ah, I had to support myself. **I had no family and so I was supporting myself** ... [22]

And to a group of pastors at a conference in 1994:

> The Lord pulled a joke on Kent State University and had me be a professor...**I had to work**—I'm not a woman's lib person—or wasn't after I got saved—so, **I had to work, I had no one to support me**. [23]

The truth is, for the first four-and-a-half years (1980-1984) that she was a professor at Kent State University, she was *legally married* to her *second* husband. By the time she left KSU, c. 1988, she was on her *third* (current) husband. It is a bold-faced *lie* that she "wasn't married" and "had no family." Her second husband was her family. The details of the second divorce, which took place while she was a KSU assistant

---

[22] Riplinger stated this during a lecture recorded at Temple Baptist Church (2100 W. Woodrow Drive, Knoxville, TN) in 1996. Sold by Mrs. Riplinger as *Riplinger Lecture Series: Research Update Q & A, Sword Slays the Dragon, King James Bible Perfection or NIV, NKJV, NASV Perversion*, A.V. Publications, Corp., P.O. Box 280, Ararat, VA 24053. It can be viewed online at http://www.archive.org/details/Questions_and_Answers_Riplinger.

[23] *Riplinger Testimony, Questions & Answers*, a pastors' conference, sold by Riplinger's A.V. Publications, Corp.

professor,[24] show Riplinger as anything but a woman claiming *not* to be "women's lib." More detail on this follow in this chapter.

It is our strong belief—as well as that of others who've spoken to us about this matter—that Riplinger hid the truth about her past *because she knew her divorces could cause an issue for her*. The kind of issue that would have quite possibly closed many church doors to her—such as those at Gospel Light Baptist Church—and greatly decreased the endorsement of King James Bible pastors who've encouraged their congregants to purchase her books.[25] And not just because she is divorced but because she is divorced *outside of scriptural rule*. If they had known about her divorces, they could have read the records and found out how she abandoned both men, something she did not want people to find out. People would have become concerned, wanting to know the truth, because they invested money into her books and materials, which they might not have if they'd known otherwise. People had the right to know the truth. Because she knew it was imperative that her divorces remain secret, she lied about her divorces when asked, in order to keep them hidden. Today, she continues on as if she has done nothing wrong. Scripture says:

> Such is the way of an adulterous woman; she eateth and wipeth her mouth, and saith, I have done no wickedness (Proverbs 30:20).

During her lecture at a pastors' conference, Riplinger said:

---

[24] Kent State University records show that she was an assistant professor from 1982 until she left around 1988.
[25] During Riplinger's first taped visit to Berean Baptist Church (4135 Thomasville Road, Winston-Salem, NC 27107), where she lectured in several church services, Senior Pastor Ronald Baity displayed some of Riplinger's books as he strongly encouraged the congregation to purchase them from Riplinger's book table.

My authority's the word of God. That's, ah—the Bible's my authority for all manners of faith and practice. [26]

Does Riplinger think she receives authority to lie from the word of God? Did she take her practice of divorce from God's word? It must be asked how she could make this claim while also bearing false witness. When one reveres God's word as their "authority," he or she will desire to live in obedience to what He says, because it matters to them. Such a person is not going to slander others, bear false witness, or write books full of misinformation. She didn't just lie to the Waites when they asked her about her divorces; she lied to every Christian who cares about God's law of marriage and to those who have funded her monetarily. Her denial enabled her to continue to glean money from faithful, unwary King James Bible believers who put their trust in her. We must question how the word of God is Gail Riplinger's "authority for all manners of faith and practice." To what "faith" and what "practice" was she referring? Saying God's word is her "authority" is a nice, pat little answer meant to sound good to her hearers.

Marriages that "Existed Only on Paper"?

It's one thing to end up divorced by no fault of one's own, such as when a spouse commits adultery, leaves with another person, or just obtains a divorce against the other's will. But it's quite another to pursue a divorce when one's spouse has *not* committed adultery (the only cause Jesus assented to) and wishes to remain married. The ground surrounding Riplinger's divorces is rocky, indeed. While both divorces are a serious matter because they were obtained outside of Scriptural grounds, the second divorce is the most controversial, as we will show in this chapter.

---

[26] *Riplinger Testimony, Question & Answer*, op. cit.

Evading the Past

In nearly every interview where she was asked to tell about herself, she would pass right over the years between childhood (lessons with a Latin tutor at the age of nine, a Roman Catholic upbringing, etc.) and the time when she became an instructor at Kent State University, often mentioning how she'd authored "six textbooks" and earned a collection of academic credentials and honorary awards. In a few places, she would mention the daughter she had when she was almost 40[27] but would rarely mention having a husband. She would avoid giving the titles of her six textbooks, because the last name of her second marriage is on them.

Having Her Daughter Answer for Her

Once the proof of her divorces became irrefutable, she chose not to acknowledge them herself. Instead, she allowed her daughter (who wasn't there all those years ago) to speak for her:

> Like many young girls, she had sought to escape a mixed-up home by establishing her own. Subsequently, she was **rejected** by not one, but two men, with whom she shared a marriage license, which **existed only on paper**. These men's physical anomaly or homosexuality, neither of which she had anticipated, deferred anything but a strained friendship, wrought with their cruelty. Before she met my father, her gracious patience had left her waiting many *years* for the return and repentance of the one, now dead, who had **abandoned her almost from the start** to pursue his homosexual lifestyle. ... What two **unsaved losers** did to her somewhere between thirty and forty years ago has virtually nothing to do with the Bible

---

[27] *Nite Line* video, featuring the *New Age Bible Versions* interview with Gail Riplinger.

version debate at hand, nor her character. [28] [Italics in original, bold text added for emphasis.]

Bryn should have verified her mother's story on her own before publicizing it. Even though she probably wants to believe her mother, God will hold her accountable for writing a false report on her behalf, because she is now an adult.

"Existed only paper" appears to imply a non-consummation of both marriages. If this is the implication intended, then there is another interesting parallel here between Riplinger and H.P. Blavatsky: Blavatsky claimed that her marriages were never consummated.[29]

The facts of Riplinger's divorces are easy to verify since public records leave a trail that tells a lot about major events in a person's life. In early 2007, due to suspicions that followed my reading of *New Age Bible Versions*, my husband and I began examining her public records. This led us to the circumstances surrounding the unscriptural nature of her divorces.

Riplinger's Allegations Against her Husbands Examined

Let us start with the first two allegations in her daughter's statement: that Gail was "rejected" by both husbands and that both marriages "existed only on paper."

---

[28] Bryn Riplinger Shutt is quoted in a letter reportedly written by Pastor Dewayne Sands of the Believer's Baptist Church of Ararat, VA. The letter was placed on the Hyles Anderson Alumni web site (HACAlumni.com) in August 2009 as a rebuttal to Pastor Jack Schaap of First Baptist Church of Hammond, IN, and Hyles-Anderson College, after he addressed the unscriptural nature of Gail Riplinger's divorces at the King James Bible Summit 2009. See note 7. Despite the claim made that Riplinger had a "mixed up home" and traumatic childhood, she never made such a claim in any interviews where she was asked to tell about herself.

[29] Ronald Pearsall, *The Table-Rappers*, 2004, by Sutton Publishing Limited, p. 211.

Gail married her first husband on June 7, 1969, in a Catholic church in Niles, Ohio,[30] becoming Gail Latessa. As a married couple, they mortgaged a home together in Youngstown, in 1973.[31] Gail's mother loaned them a nice sum for their down payment.[32] Together they financed a Chevrolet Vega, accrued credit balances with the Strouss Department Store, and purchased household furnishings and appliances.[33] They lived together during their marriage, which clearly did not exist "only on paper." If a "physical anomaly"— especially one that causes non-consummation—or "homosexuality" forces a marriage to exist "only on paper" then that is what an annulment is designed for. In Ohio, Gail could have obtained an annulment at any time during the first two years of her marriage,[34] yet she did not.

On October 17, 1974, five years into the marriage, Gail filed a Complaint for Divorce with the Mahoning County Court of Common

---

[30] Marriage record No. 61989, Terry Latessa and Gail Anne Ludwig, June 7, 1969, Niles, Ohio. On file at the Trumbull County Probate Court, 161 High St., Warren, Ohio 44481-1230, http://www.trumbullprobate.org/.

[31] According to the Separation Agreement in their divorce file (see endnote 35), the house was financed through the First Federal Savings and Loan Association of Youngstown, Ohio. Mahoning County deed records show they purchased the home in 1973.

[32] According to the Separation Agreement in their divorce file (see endnote 35), the amount is listed as $14,000, a lot of money in 1969. As part of the Separation Agreement, the money had to be paid back to Gail's mother when the house was sold following the divorce.

[33] According to the Separation Agreement in their divorce file, they accrued these items together while living in the same house.

[34] Ohio Code Section 3105.31-32 allows the annulment of a marriage when either party is under age, has a previous undissolved marriage, is mentally incompetent, obtained by fraud or force the consent to marry, or when the marriage was never consummated. There are time limits for each of the grounds for annulment. It appears that Riplinger is claiming non-consummation with her allegations of "rejection" and "physical anomaly." Since 1963, Ohio law has allowed annulments within the first two years of a marriage for the reason of non-consummation. Code section can be viewed at *Lawriter Ohio Laws and Rules*: http://codes.ohio.gov/orc/3105.31 and http://codes.ohio.gov/orc/3105.32.

Pleas. She also obtained an order for Legal Separation.[35] Legal Separation is an arrangement, through court order, that permits two people to live apart from each other while still married. Obviously, there is no need to tell the court you want to live separate from your husband unless you've been living with him. As previously mentioned, this took place after the age of 26, the age at which Riplinger has said in several public places she was "saved."

On February 10, 1975, just under four months after filing, the divorce became final.[36] She made no complaint of adultery or abandonment by Mr. Latessa as her reason for wanting the divorce.[37] In other words, she had no scriptural allowance. The proceeds from their house, which had been sold previously, were used to pay off their accrued debt.[38] Gail moved back into the house in which she'd grown up, in Niles, Ohio, where her mother still lived.[39]

Gail's Second Marriage

---

[35] Divorce Record Case No. 74-DR-1543, *Gail Anne Latessa v. Terry Latessa*, February 10, 1975, including detailed Separation Agreement. On file at Mahoning County Court, Clerk of Courts, 120 Market St., 2nd Floor, Youngstown, OH 44503,
www.mahoningcountyoh.gov/MahoningWeb/Department+and+Agencies/Department/Probate+Court/.
[36] Ibid.
[37] Ibid.
[38] Ibid.
[39] Ibid. Riplinger listed this as her home address on record of marriage to Mr. Latessa and on her Complaint for Divorce, February 10, 1975. After her mother's death, the house was sold in 1982.

Gail's second marriage took place a year and nine months later, in Liberty, Portage County, Ohio, on November 5, 1976, when she became Gail Kaleda.⁴⁰ At the time, she was a fulltime undergraduate student at KSU, working toward a B.A. in Interior Design. Her husband, Frank, supported them, working as a retail manager.⁴¹, ⁴² They moved into a mobile home park near KSU's main campus in Kent, Ohio.⁴³ The location was convenient for Gail who, in the summer of 1980, was appointed by KSU to the position of Instructor in the then titled Home Economics Department.⁴⁴ On February 12, 1981, she and Frank formed a non-profit educational, philanthropic corporation with the Ohio Secretary of State, which they named *Truth and Life*. On the registration paperwork, Gail and her husband listed their home address as their

---

⁴⁰ Marriage record No. 45789, Docket 84, page 89, Frank A. Kaleda and Gail Anne Ludwig, November 5, 1976, Portage County, Ohio. On file at the Portage County Probate Court, 203 W. Main St., 2nd Floor, P.O. Box 936, Ravenna, Ohio 44266 http://www.portageco.com/ misc_countyrecords.htm. Wedding photos of Gail and her second husband courtesy of Mr. Kaleda's family.
⁴¹ Ibid. The record indicates Gail's occupation as "student" and her husband's as "retail manager."
⁴² According to Kent State University alumni records, Gail was nearly halfway through her four-year B.A. degree in Interior Design. Commencement records list her in the graduating class for Interior Design, June 1978. All alumni records can be viewed in the Archive Department of the Kent State University Library.
⁴³ Today, the name of this mobile home park is Whispering Pines.
⁴⁴ In 1983, the Kent State University Home Economics department was renamed Family and Consumer Studies.

lot number in the mobile home park.⁴⁵ This is just one of several records showing that Mr. Kaleda did not abandon Gail "almost from the start" of their eight-year marriage. A neighbor who knew them for several years states they appeared as "any happy, normal married couple."⁴⁶

In addition to the paperwork for the non-profit corporation, that same year the Kaledas filed a mortgage and a warranty deed together for the purchase of a newly built home in the Brookside Farm subdivision of Kent, Ohio.⁴⁷, ⁴⁸ On July 17, 1981, the couple obtained a mortgage together with the AmeriTrust Company of Portage County.⁴⁹ A notary public declared that the couple appeared on that date to sign the mortgage paperwork.⁵⁰ Then on July 30, 1981, they purchased the house from the W & J Development Company, Inc., with their names listed *together* as Grantee.⁵¹ According to paperwork, in March 1982, the Kaledas paid the mortgage in full. Two months later, Gail, the only child of her parents⁵² and sole named Executrix of her deceased

---

⁴⁵ Ohio Secretary of State Charter/Registration Number 569156, TRUTH AND LIFE, registered February 12, 1981. Home address listed by the Kaledas was 1915 State Route 59, lot #8 (in the now named Whispering Pines Mobile Home Park), Kent, Ohio. The purpose of the group was most likely to satisfy Kent State University's continuing education requirements for the reappointment of faculty, on which Gail was a newly hired Instructor. KSU requires, among other things, service to the community by its faculty, as a requirement for reappointment each year. Truth and Life remained registered for two years after the divorce.
⁴⁶ This former neighbor of the Kaleda's asked to remain anonymous.
⁴⁷ The AmeriTrust Company of Kent, Ohio, granted an open-end mortgage to Frank and Gail Kaleda, listed as "husband and wife," on July 17, 1981. The house was a 2,000- square-foot bi-level, built in 1979.
⁴⁸ Warrantee Deed: W & J Development Company, Inc., Grantor, to Frank A. Kaleda and Gail A. Kaleda, Grantee, July 30, 1981, Kent, Portage County, Ohio.
⁴⁹ See mortgage information, note 32.
⁵⁰ Ibid.
⁵¹ See Warrantee Deed information, note 33.
⁵² NiteLine features *New Age Bible Versions* (video), an interview with Gail Riplinger, c. 1995, Dove Broadcasting, Inc., P.O. Box 1616, Greenville, SC 29602. Gail told the hostess of the program that she "was an only child." The

mother's estate, transferred her mother's house to new owners,[53] acquiring any available proceeds.

On April 25, 1984, Gail entered a Complaint for Divorce followed by a lengthy Separation Agreement.[54] If her husband had truly abandoned her, as her daughter claims on her behalf, a Legal Separation would have been unnecessary since a Legal Separation is for spouses who have been living together. The following day, her husband was served with divorce papers and forced to vacate their home.[55] Obviously, he would not have been forced to vacate their home if he had abandoned her near the start of their marriage and left her waiting for his return. The divorce record clearly indicates they lived together at the same address (same house) when he was forced to leave.[56] Once again, Gail did not state adultery, abandonment, non-consummation, or homosexuality as her reason for wanting the divorce.

On July 3, 1984, the husband's attorney wrote a letter to the Court in which he stated concern for his client:

> [Mr. Kaleda] states he wishes to withdraw his answer and counterclaim in Case No. 84 CV 0652 for personal reasons – **he wishes to remain married to his wife, Gail Kaleda**, and that neither his wife nor he wish to contest this matter further. **I do not think this is true that the wife does not wish to contest the matter.** His wife insisted upon accompanying

---

divorce record of her parent declares she was the only child born during their marriage, on file in Franklin County, Ohio.

[53] Deed of Fiduciary, Statutory Form, record number 41195, May 11, 1982, City of Niles, Trumbull County, Ohio; "Gail Ludwig Latessa Kaleda as Executrix of the Estate of Helen Ludwig, deceased."

[54] Divorce Record Case No. 84-CV-0652, *Gail Ludwig Kaleda v. Frank Kaleda*, August 6, 1984, including detailed Separation Agreement. On file at Portage County Common Pleas, Clerk of Courts, P.O. Box 1035, Ravenna, OH 44266, http://www.co.portage.oh.us/clerkofcourts.htm, http://www.portageco.com/misc_countyrecords.htm

[55] Ibid.

[56] Ibid.

him into my office and staying with him during our office conference. **I asked if she was going to contest this matter any further and she said it was none of my business...**[57] [Emphasis added.]

As the court documents attest, it is simply implausible that both husbands rejected or abandoned Gail throughout either marriage. She clearly purchased and shared homes with both husbands. And the second husband stated he wished to remain married to her, which shows he did not abandon her "almost from the start" of the marriage and never return to her.[58] And since he didn't abandon her, it is impossible that she waited "many *years* for [his] return and repentance." She was married to Mr. Kaleda for eight years and then married her current husband just two months after divorcing him.

No matter the reason for why Gail ended each marriage, they were still real marriages and the divorces are real divorces.

On to the third allegation: "These men's physical anomaly or homosexuality." This is a very serious charge and one refuted by the evidence already presented. First, Bryn Riplinger Shutt is not qualified to make such claims against these men on behalf of her mother, since she knows absolutely nothing about them on a personal level and has obviously not examined the details of her mother's divorce and marriage records. Second, Riplinger did not make a claim of *homosexuality*, or even *adultery*, by either husband when she filed for divorce. She made no claim of any variety of sexual unfaithfulness against either husband.

The first husband is currently living with a woman who is a former schoolmate of Gail. When this girlfriend was recently asked if Mr. Latessa has any sort of "anomaly" or is a homosexual, her response was hearty laughter. In her view, such allegations are

---

[57] Ibid.
[58] Ibid.

preposterous. Her answer speaks volumes against Riplinger's attempts to malign her husbands through false accusation.

If it were true that the second husband had abandoned her "almost from the start" of their marriage to pursue a homosexual lifestyle, she could have obtained an annulment with ease, within the first two years of the marriage, and been free to go. But she did not and, instead, remained married for eight years, living with him[59] as already shown in this chapter. Instead of "homosexuality," she stated, "extreme cruelty" (a very vague interpretation) and "gross neglect of duty" (another vague, open-ended claim) on the Complaint for Divorce.[60] Such unscriptural "complaints" are provided by the worldly Ohio court system, which holds little respect for God's law on marriage. Although separation for a time and plenty of marital counseling with their pastor[61] would have been a positive and permissible action to help repair and strengthen their marriage, Riplinger's reasons for the divorce were outside Scriptural grounds. Scripture says:

> And [he] said, for this cause shall a man leave father and mother, and shall cleave to his wife: and **they twain shall be one flesh**? Wherefore they are no more twain,

---

[59] The second marriage went from November 1976 to August 1984, when the divorce was finalized, just three months short of eight years.

[60] Divorce Record Case No. 84-CV-0652, *Gail Ludwig Kaleda v. Frank Kaleda*, August 6, 1984, including detailed Separation Agreement. On file at Portage County Common Pleas, Clerk of Courts, P.O. Box 1035, Ravenna, OH 44266, http://www.co.portage.oh.us/clerkofcourts.htm, http://www.portageco.com/misc_countyrecords.htm

[61] According to a former acquaintance of the Kaledas, the couple attended the Christian Life Center Assembly of God church in Kent, Ohio, and then eventually began attending Grace Baptist Church next door, in the late 1970s and early 1980s. Both churches are locally known for their dedicated ministries of reaching out to students of Kent State University. Gail had at least two pastors available upon whom she could have called for Scriptural guidance and counsel concerning her second marriage, in lieu of divorce.

but one flesh. **What therefore God hath joined together, let not man put asunder** (Matthew 19:5-6).

And if a woman shall put away her husband, and be married to another, **she committeth adultery** (Mark 10:12).

And unto the married I command, yet not I, but the Lord, **Let not the wife depart from her husband: But and if she depart, let her remain unmarried, or be reconciled to her husband** ... The wife is **bound by the law** as long as her husband liveth; but if her husband be dead, she is at liberty to be married to whom she will; only in the Lord (1 Corinthians 7:10-11, 39).

Wives, **submit yourselves unto your own husbands**, as unto the Lord (Ephesians 5:22).

Therefore as the church is subject unto Christ, so **let the wives be [subject] to their own husbands** in every thing (Ephesians 5:24).

Wives, **submit yourselves unto your own husbands**, as it is fit in the Lord (Colossians 3:18).

According to 1 Corinthians 7:39, the wife who departs from her husband is allowed to remarry *only* if her husband is dead. Remarrying while he is alive not only makes her an adulteress but it also makes her current husband guilty of adultery. This is because God made marriage to be a permanent covenant, for life. Has God's word become outdated? To Riplinger's defenders, are these verses irrelevant or obsolete? Was God just kidding when He spoke these words to Paul? No, these are serious words meant for a serious matter. To God, marriage is a very serious commitment. It is a covenant. Even if Gail could have somehow been right in obtaining her divorces as a professing Christian, she was not allowed to remarry.

> For the woman which hath an husband is bound by the law to her husband as long as he liveth…(Romans 7:2a-3)
>
> The wife is bound by the law as long as her husband liveth…So then if, **while her husband liveth, she be married to another man, she shall be called an adulteress**…(1 Corinthians 7:39) [62]

Does God have to say it more than once? These verses are written to Christians and, as difficult as it may be to accept, it is saying that a woman will be "called an adulteress" for as long as her husband *liveth* (continual present tense verb). This is because marriage is permanent, for life. A person who is saved will not lose his or her salvation for living in adultery but they are certainly disqualified from leadership in the church. An adulteress is one with her lawful (original), living husband, according to God's law, while also married to another man who is not her lawful husband. She has perverted the bond of oneness in the covenant of marriage. God is so very serious about the oneness and permanence of marriage because it is the model of Christ and the church, which is why He hates and does not accept divorce. If He were not serious about it, it would be permissible for Christians to get divorced then remarry, repent, then get divorced again, remarry and repent again, and so on, as if divorce is not a problem. Christians who live in continual disobedience are chastened by the Lord, which can

---

[62] Gail Riplinger lived in adultery against her second husband for 15 years after the divorce, and at least six years of that time occurred during the late 1980s and through the 1990s, when she was most active writing her books and teaching in church pulpits. Her first husband is still living, 41 years later. 1 Cor. 7:39 says that while a woman's husband is still living and she has left him and married another man, *she shall be called an adulteress*. When Dr. D.A. Waite and his wife first asked Gail if she had been divorced twice in the past, she denied she had ever been married to anyone other than her current (third) husband, Mike. It is most likely that Gail Riplinger covered her divorces because she feared how the knowledge of them would affect her popularity among KJV pastors and adherents and the successful sales of her books.

mean illness, suffering, and even physical death. God chastens every "son" that is His (Heb 12:5-11).

Lastly, does the above picture appear to be that of a woman embarking on a marriage that was merely a "strained friendship"? Or does Gail look rather happy and cozy with Mr. Kaleda? Does Mr. Kaleda look like a deserting homosexual or a man happy to kiss his wife on his wedding day?

Riplinger continues to be invited to churches by pastors who feign obedience to God's word while ignoring what it says. God does not take Gail's divorces lightly, nor her hiding them and then lying about them, as do some pastors who continue to defend her instead of calling her to honesty and repentance.

As for the fourth, and final, allegation against her husbands: "What two unsaved losers did to her…" Gail's first husband, Mr. Latessa, was a Roman Catholic,[63] something she knew when she married him, since she too was a Roman Catholic.[64] Leaving the Roman Catholic Church at "the age of 26," as she has stated several times, did not give her permission to begin referring to him in such an

---

[63] Marriage record No. 61989, Terry Latessa and Gail Anne Ludwig, June 7, 1969, Niles, Ohio. On file at the Trumbull County Probate Court, 161 High St., Warren, Ohio 44481-1230, http://www.trumbullprobate.org/. The record indicates the Latessas were married by Father Masciangelo, at the Our Lady of Mount Carmel Catholic Church of Niles, Ohio. Mr. Latessa attended the Our Lady of Mount Carmel Catholic High School, which was affiliated with the church.

[64] During her testimony in a lecture taped at Temple Baptist Church (2100 W. Woodrow Drive, Knoxville, TN) in 1996, Gail stated she was a Catholic until she was 26-years-old. Video sold by Mrs. Riplinger as *Riplinger Lecture Series: Research Update Q & A, Sword Slays the Dragon, King James Bible Perfection or NIV, NKJV, NASV Perversion*, A.V. Publications, Corp., P.O. Box 280, Ararat, VA 24053. Can be viewed online at http://www.archive.org/details/Questions_and_Answers_Riplinger.

uncharitable manner. "Loser" or not, she chose to marry him. After the time that she says she was saved, she chose *not* to stay with her "unsaved" husband and fulfill 1 Peter 3:1:

> Likewise, ye **wives, be in subjection to your own husbands**; that, if any obey not the word, **they also may without the word be won by the conversation [Christian example] of the wives**.

Just because a woman decides years later that the man she married is a "loser" does not justify obtaining a divorce. Jesus certainly never gave an allowance for Christians to divorce their spouses for being "unsaved losers." What an unkind, un-Christ-like thing for a woman to say of people she believes are on their way to hell. We believe her lack of love for these two men is apparent in the way she speaks of them today.

As for the second husband, Mr. Kaleda, there are former acquaintances who attest that he was a Christian. Before he was saved, he was a practitioner of New Age philosophy and mysticism.[65] He studied and taught Transcendental Meditation (TM) in the mid 1970s and then renounced it after becoming born again.[66] He then wrote an exposé titled *The Shining Ones*[67] in which he revealed the secret mantras that are given to TM initiates.[68] In fact, Riplinger herself,

---

[65] Frank Kaleda, *The Shining Ones*. Privately published in Kent, Ohio, 1978, as cited in *Levitation, What is It, How it Works, How to Do It*, by Steve Richards, The Aquarian Press, 1980, pp. 22 and 65. Richards also writes: "One instructor [Frank Kaleda], now out of the movement, recalls: 'I frequently experienced the sensation of becoming gaseous, first filling the room, then expanding over the Mediterranean Sea (while in Spain), and finally extending throughout the universe.'" *Levitation*, p. 13.
[66] Ibid.
[67] Ibid.
[68] Ibid. Richards writes: "Says Mr. Kaleda of Ohio: 'Other advanced techniques may be used, but of six initiators questioned, it was always the [mantra] prefix *Shri* and the suffix *Namah*.'" *Levitation*, p. 66. And in Francisco Di Biase and Mario Sergio F. da Rocha, *Caminhos Da Cura*, p. 20, published in Portuguese online at

when speaking at a pastors' conference about this same period in her life, said:

> Before I was saved, I was reading a lot of material relating to the New Age movement and I was what you might call, at that time, a New Ager…**I was reading some of the Hindu mystics,** I was reading Sri Aurobindo, **I was initiated into Transcendental Meditation…** [69]

It is our belief that she and Mr. Kaleda met at or near Kent State University, through their mutual interest in Eastern mysticism and Transcendental Meditation.

One of Mr. Kaleda's former TM students (from 1975), Ron, met him while attending KSU and remembers Mr. Kaleda as "dedicated" to whatever he was doing at any particular time and an "honorable" person. Ron said Mr. Kaleda gave "free" classes. He saw Mr. Kaleda several years later (around 1978) and found out "he had become a born again Christian and was dedicated to his new path [Christianity]."[70]

---

http://www.tumicse.com.br/phpBB2/download.php?id=129&sid=807e5d153f59aca622fb7fedb7a4546e, on p. 20, in the paragraph mentioning Frank Kaleda, the English translation reads: "In the final two years of the 70s and the first two years of the 80s, dissident instructors of TM [Transcendental Mediation], such as **Frank Kaleda**, Susan Scott, John Weldon, and Zola Levitt, **came to publicly divulge the mantras of TM**. We knew there were only sixteen mantras that were given to initiates, according to their age group. Our own clinical experience [with TM] confirms the accuracy of the information divulged by these dissidents." (Emphasis added.)

[69] Sri Aurobindo, and Indian nationalist and yogi, believed in the "evolving soul." His best known writings "include, in prose, *The Life Divine*, considered his single great work of metaphysics, *The Synthesis of Yoga, Secrets of the Vedas, Essays on the Gita, The Human Cycle, The Ideal of Human Unity, Renaissance in India and other essays, Supramental Manifestation upon Earth, The Future Poetry, Thoughts and Aphorisms* and several volumes of letters." Source: Wikipedia, "Sri Aurobindo," http://en.wikipedia.org/wiki/Sri_Aurobindo.]

[70] To protect the privacy of this former student of Frank Kaleda, his real name has been changed.

When I asked Ron if he recalls whether Mr. Kaleda had ever been a homosexual, he said he was never aware of such.

Another former acquaintance, Jim, who knew the Kaledas from church, in the late 1970s, stated he knew Mr. Kaleda as a Christian.[71] In the divorce Separation Agreement, there is a reference to Mr. Kaleda's "Ministry materials."[72] For Gail Riplinger, it seems easy to slander a man when he's unable to defend himself because he's dead. Mr. Kaleda's turning away from his Eastern mystical practices speaks volumes about a changed life, which comes from believing on Jesus Christ as one's Savior.

Whether one or both husbands were unsaved, Riplinger had no scriptural excuse for divorcing them.

> And the woman which hath an husband that believeth not, and **if he be pleased to dwell with her, let her not leave him.** (1 Corinthians 7:13)

Gail left both of her husbands; they did not leave her. The second husband stated his wish to remain married to her, yet she kicked him out of their home, sold the home, divorced him, took back her maiden name (as if that somehow removes the permanence of marriage), and then married her current husband two months later. Does Gail Riplinger have some kind of leeway that no other Christian has? No. Why, then, are there still some pastors rallying to her defense while ignoring the fact that she has not personally acknowledged or apologized publicly of her lying to cover up what she knew people deserved to know the moment she came onto the King James Bible scene?

---

[71] To project the privacy of this former acquaintance, their name has been changed. This acquaintance attended the Christian Life Center Assembly of God in Kent, Ohio (see endnote 45), with the Kaledas until they left to attend the Grace Baptist Church, next door.

[72] Divorce Record Case No. 84-CV-0652, *Gail Ludwig Kaleda v. Frank Kaleda*, August 6, 1984, including detailed Separation Agreement. On file at Portage County Common Pleas, Clerk of Courts, P.O. Box 1035, Ravenna, OH 44266, http://www.co.portage.oh.us/clerkofcourts.htm, http://www.portageco.com/misc_countyrecords.htm

Keeping the Cover on Controversy

"Every wise woman buildeth her house:
but the foolish plucketh it down with her hands."
    – Proverbs 14:1

Now, on to the most likely reason why Gail kept her divorces a secret, following her debut in the King James Bible world: the highly controversial circumstances surrounding her second divorce and third (current) marriage.

In a well-publicized interview, conducted in 1995 by Mrs. Yvonne Waite, Riplinger stated that she knew her current husband, Michael Riplinger, for a year prior to marrying him.[73] This means she met him somewhere around six to eight months before she filed for her divorce from her second husband, Mr. Kaleda. What were she and Mr. Riplinger doing while she was married to another man? What were they doing that cultivated enough feelings between them to get married so soon after she divorced Mr. Kaleda? Whatever it was, it must have been enough to make her confident to marry him just two months after divorcing her second husband, as will be explained in the following sections.

Gail Kaleda Met Michael Riplinger While Still Married to Mr. Kaleda

"Stolen waters are sweet, and bread eaten in secret is pleasant." –Proverbs 9:17

"For the lips of a strange woman [an adulteress] drop as an honeycomb,
and her mouth is smoother than oil: But her end is as wormwood,
sharp as a twoedged sword. Her feet go down to death; her steps
take hold on hell." –Proverbs 5:1-5

---

[73] *Riplinger's Testimony, Question & Answer, Interview* with Mrs. Yvonne Waite, after a pastors' conference in NC, April 1995. Riplinger sells this interview in her A.V. Publications catalog.

Gail met her current husband, Michael, while she was still married to her second husband. Michael's sister was attending Kent State University, working on her B.F.A. (Bachelor of Fine Arts) at the same time that Gail was a graduate student (obtaining her M.F.A.) and an Instructor there,[74] and the two women knew each other. The interview that Riplinger did with Mrs. Waite in 1995 sheds much light on the facts of the matter. Mrs. Waite asked Gail how she met Michael, and this was her answer:

> Ah, **one of my students** became a Christian; I led her to the Lord. And **she had a brother** that had never been married. And **she started praying that her brother would meet someone like me**. That's all she said, that he'd meet someone like me—I don't know why, you know, she thought I was all right, or whatever, but. And, so, he, he—she moved away, and **his mother invited me over to dinner at their house and I went over. And, ah, I met him**.[75]

Riplinger's words indicate the willful agreement of a married woman to go to someone's house with the intention of being introduced to another man. Married women who meet other men appear on the Jerry Springer and Dr. Phil shows.

Mrs. Waite asked Gail if she "fell in love" with Michael and married him "right off the bat," and Riplinger answered:

> Well, I think it was **within a year, or something like that, that, ah, we were married**. ... But the Lord is—He has His

---

[74] Alice J. Riplinger is listed in the *Kent State University Alumni Directory*, 2002, Harris Publishing. We confirmed she is Michael's sister via their father's (Carl Riplinger) obituary in the Akron Beacon Journal from November 19, 1994. She is listed as obtaining a B.F.A. in Crafts in 1984. She graduated the same year (1984) that Gail Riplinger left her second husband and married Michael Riplinger.

[75] *Testimony* interview with Mrs. Waite, 1995. Sold in Riplinger's A.V. Publications catalog.

timing, and it just breaks my heart when I see people not waiting for the Lord's timing on things, you know? [76]

Interestingly, Riplinger never answered the part about falling in love. However, by her own admission, she met Michael months before she divorced Mr. Kaleda, since "a year" before she and Michael married would have been October 1983, with the divorce from Mr. Kaleda becoming final in August 1984, just two months before their marriage. She completely forgot to tell Mrs. Waite that she divorced her second husband just two months prior to marrying Michael. She did not say a word about still being married to Mr. Kaleda when she went to Michael's mother's house to meet Michael, although, for some reason, she emphasized that Michael had never been married, as if this was somehow meant give a false or subliminal impression that she too had never been married. Surely, Mr. Kaleda was not also invited to this dinner. What was Gail doing meeting another man at his mother's house a good six months before she filed for divorce (April 1984) from her husband? Her words give the false impression that Michael is her first husband. All lies.

She had the audacity to give "the Lord" credit for bringing Michael into her life. How blasphemous to say that God brought her a man for whom she abandoned her spouse. "The Lord" had *nothing* to do with her meeting and marrying Michael Riplinger nor her choice to abandon and commit adultery against Mr. Kaleda. Riplinger does not speak of the God of the Bible, Who never grants permission to sin. She spoke of another "God," one of whom the scripture warns: the "god of this world" and "Father of lies," who deceives the simple and the proud.

A Husband Spurned

Gail's complaint for divorce states: "[within the last ten (10) days] the living conditions in the parties [sic] home have been intolerable and ...

---

[76] Ibid.

subjects the Plaintiff [Gail] to grave danger and places her in fear of her safety." What made Mr. Kaleda become so upset? It is highly probable that he had discovered his wife was seeing another man. Gail neglected to tell the court about that technicality. No doubt she ignited the situation, disobeying both God and her husband until she set herself up as the justifiable victim and then pleaded to the State of Ohio to grant her a divorce.[77] Did Mr. Kaleda become so upset because Gail told him she was leaving him for Michael? Did she expect Mr. Kaleda to just *understand* that his wife wanted to kick him out of their home and abandon him for another man? Does God's word warn for nothing: "For jealousy is the rage of a man [husband]: therefore he will not spare in the day of vengeance. He will not regard [accept] any ransom [compensation]; neither will he rest content, though thou givest many gifts (Proverbs 6:35)"? Few men take kindly to another man taking away their wife. While a stolen vase can be returned or replaced, that which is stolen through adultery cannot be. The divorce record does not indicate that Gail had called the police or filed a report with them when this supposed incident took place.

---

[77] Once one gets the full picture of Gail Riplinger's hidden life and all the evil details that pertain to it, it becomes rather clear that she is one who believes she gets what she wants, even if she must play the victim to sway people's emotions to her favor. The details of the divorce record show a woman with a premeditated plan, who decided beforehand to find a way to justify obtaining a divorce from her husband so that she would be free to marry the next one (whom she already knew for nearly a year) just as soon as the divorce became final. Her playing the victim by claiming violence on the part of her spurned husband ensured that the court would grant her a restraining order and have Mr. Kaleda kicked out of their home immediately, enabling her to proceed with the divorce, sell the house and further her plans. Less than a month after the divorce became final, she and Michael Riplinger filed for a marriage license at the Summit County courthouse, marrying one month later. Her hidden life is the picture of a calculating woman who does what she wishes and it does not matter who she hurts or manipulates along the way. Hiding her real self and her wicked past, she has done what is necessary to manipulate people into believing that she is someone she is not, and into buying her books and making her a rich woman. Those who are able to *see* the full picture become free of Gail Riplinger and her teachings. Praise God!

No wonder Mr. Kaleda told the court, in his counterclaim, that:

> He has always fulfilled his marital obligations during the parties' marriage, but that the Plaintiff [Gail] has not been a dutiful wife and has been guilty of gross neglect of duty and extreme cruelty…

In addition, the court record states that Mr. Kaleda testified that Gail's accusation of violence toward her, "extreme cruelty," and "gross neglect of duty" were false. It appears that Mr. Kaleda had found out that his wife was being unfaithful and was falsely accusing him in order to sway the court in her favor, to grant her the divorce. In other words, did Gail make up the story about feeling threatened so that the court would favor her and give her the divorce? At any rate, the record shows that Mr. Kaleda resided at the couple's home and that he had not abandoned Gail early on in their marriage, as she is now claiming.

Jesus' Rules for Marriage and Divorce Have not Changed

He said:

> And if a woman shall put away her husband, and be married to another, she **committeth** adultery (Mark 10:12). [78]

---

[78] The word *committeth* is a verb in the present tense, meaning that a woman is presently committing adultery if she has divorced her husband and married another. This means a continual (ongoing) action (Greek: *Moichao*, meaning "to have unlawful intercourse, the *ongoing* act of committing adultery"), lasting for as long as she is married to another man who is not her legal husband, until her legal husband dies. Gail Riplinger may have finally stopped committing adultery against her second husband when he died in 1999 but her first husband is still living. The reason she is required to stop lying about her divorces and husbands is because lying and slander are sins; and the reason she is required to apologize publicly to those she has lied to is because she had two husbands still living during the time when she was visiting churches and trying to sell her initial books throughout the 1990s—and the first husband is still living, nearly 40 years later. If she were truly repentant and apologetic before God's people, she would not still be trying to hide her divorces and

> So then if, while her husband **liveth**, she be married to another man, **she shall be called an adulteress** (Romans 7:3a) [79]

Have Jesus' words expired over the last two millennia? Did He mean them for everyone except Gail Riplinger? No. The meaning of His words is that Gail Riplinger will continue to be an adulteress until her first husband dies. Besides being a woman, this continuing state of sexual sin (and lying about it) disqualifies Gail Riplinger from teaching or having any position of authority in the church.

Paul reinforced Jesus' words:

> So then if, while her husband liveth, she be married to another man, she shall be called an adulteress (Romans 7:3).

Are the pastors who continue to defend her, despite God having the final word, calling God's word a liar?

The Other Man

Did Michael's sister not know that her instructor, Gail Kaleda, was a married woman? Riplinger says she "led her to the Lord." Really? Why did Miss Riplinger tell Gail that she wanted her brother to marry someone like her? Are we to think that Gail's "Christian" future sister-in-law wished her never-married brother to marry an already-married woman who did not value faithfulness to her husband? Did the newly saved Miss Riplinger understand that God calls that *adultery*? Why did

---

would have no problem acknowledging them. According to God's word, in several places, she is continuing to commit adultery while married to another man.

[79] Ibid. Just as *committeth* is a present tense verb, so is the word *liveth*. While her husband is alive, she shall be called an adulteress. Besides being a woman, this disqualifies Gail Riplinger from teaching or having any position of authority in the church.

her mentor, Mrs. Kaleda, not explain that to her? Did Michael's mother know Gail was married? Did Gail hide that fact?

Why did Michael Riplinger not avoid having anything to do with another man's wife? He is not unlike the young man devoid of understanding in Proverbs 7. In Proverbs 6:20-35 God gravely warns:

> For by means of a whorish woman [literally, "unfaithful wife"] a man is brought to a piece of bread: and **the adulteress will hunt for [his] precious life**. Can a man take fire in his bosom, and his clothes not be burned? Can one go upon hot coals, and his feet not be burned? **So he that goeth in to his neighbour's wife; whosoever toucheth her shall not be innocent** (Proverbs 6:26-29). [80]

Jesus said:

> Whosoever shall marry her that is divorced committeth adultery (Matthew 5:32).

In the interview it is almost *ironic* that Gail refers to Michael as "precious" several times. God says the adulteress hunts for the "*precious* life." Did Michael Riplinger not realize this when he took another man's wife? Did he not realize he was taking his neighbor's wife, that which did not belong to him? Was Michael duped into believing that Gail was a victim who wanted out of her marriage? For certain, he was a marital interloper. The word "committeth" in Matthew 5:32 is in the present tense (ongoing).

---

[80] Is the real reason why Gail Riplinger shows such disdain for the NIV because it minces no words when plainly addressing the adulterous woman and man: "So is he who sleeps with another man's wife; no one who touches her will go unpunished (Proverbs 6:29)."

A Clever Disguise

Unfortunately, Mrs. Waite did not know the *real* Gail Riplinger when she interviewed her in 1995. How could she, or anyone else, have known her when Riplinger so carefully and cleverly passed herself off as someone she was not? During the interview Mrs. Waite complemented Riplinger, saying, "You're very beautiful…I don't know what I had expected, although Dr. James Sightler had said that you were a picture of what a Christian woman should look like and act like, which was very nice…I think when men meet you, they probably are taken back a little because they probably expect sort of a feminist-looking person, and you're feminine and you appear to be very dear." The key words here are "you appear to be." Riplinger *appears* to be kind, nice, sweet, soft-spoken, and "Christian." She has the outward semblance of that which she knows she must appear as in order to warm her way into people's churches and trust, yet her fruit is clearly contrary to God's word. She seems to know how to grasp the confidence of people who trust her, interspersing her speech with quotations of scripture and terminology well recognized by Christians. She is *very good* at what she does. If she had come across as the feminist, husband-bashing adulteress that her past clearly shows, she would not have had a chance in an ice age of selling a single book or even receiving one invitation to speak to someone's church congregation. How clever she is. Shame on Dr. Sightler for endorsing Riplinger simply because she claims to share his beliefs on the KJV! A person should be required to share more than just a doctrinal belief in order to prove that they are a genuine, trustworthy person, and before they are granted any prominence in the church.

God says:

> As a jewel of gold in a swine's snout, so is a fair woman which is without discretion [moral perception] (Proverbs 11:22).

Of Riplinger's false image and deceit in covering the truth about her life and marriage to Michael Riplinger, God says:

> The lip of truth shall be established for ever: but a lying tongue is but for a moment. Deceit is in the heart of them that imagine evil...Lying lips are abomination to the LORD: but they that deal truly are his delight (Proverbs 12:19-20a, 22).

Gail Riplinger was not "dealing truly" as she hid her past and who she is, and she continues in her deceit as she refuses to apologize to the many people whom she has lied to over the past 17 years. Does God's word apply to everyone but Gail Riplinger?

Appearances are often deceiving and it would be best if we Christians started to fully understand what that means. Did Jesus warn the church concerning sneaky wolves in sheep's clothing because He was bored or just wanted something about which to talk, or because it is a threat that is very real? The wolf wears sheep's clothing so that the sheep will not recognize him/her. *Do we get it?* It is the same with any unqualified person who comes into the church attempting to make us believe they are Godly, sweet, and wonderful. And just because a person claims they love God's word does not mean they truly do. The real test is whether they OBEY God's word. We *must* examine their fruit.

By now, it seems clear that Gail Riplinger has a difficult time telling the truth. It just does not seem to be very important to her. The most contentious problem in this divorce-remarriage fiasco is Riplinger allowing her daughter to spread wicked lies about her mother's first two husbands, as well as Gail's continuance in refusing to acknowledge her deceit in covering up her past because she knew that God-fearing, Bible-believing folks with strong family values would have been more Berean-minded, had they known.

A Second Divorce and then a Third Marriage Just Two Months Later

When one looks at Gail's second divorce record, it becomes clear that she was in quite a hurry to divorce Mr. Kaleda and move on with Mike Riplinger. In the early fall of 1983 she was newly graduated with a M.F.A. (her highest degree),[81] teaching courses in Interior Design at KSU,[82] when she was introduced to Michael Riplinger, a Sears repairman from Akron, Ohio, who could "fix anything."[83]

Planning to Move On

Already acquainted with Michael Riplinger for close to half a year,[84] Gail put her ducks cleverly in a row, deciding she no longer wanted to remain married to Frank Kaleda. On April 25, 1984, she filed for divorce and requested the Court allow her to keep their house, with an estimated property value of $65,000, free and clear from any interest of her husband, a request that was granted to her.[85] Although Mr. Kaleda stated in writing and to his attorney that he wished to remain married

---

[81] *Kent State University Convocation for Graduate Candidates*, August 20, 1983. She is listed as Gail Kaleda under Master of Fine Arts: Art. This was her terminal degree for her Interior Design major.

[82] Gail is listed (as Gail L. Kaleda and then Gail K. Ludwig) in the Kent State University course bulletins beginning as an Instructor in 1980 and then moving up one rank to become an Assistant Professor in 1984. The highest faculty rank she achieved at KSU was that of Assistant Professor. In each bulletin she is listed in the Family and Consumer Studies Department (formerly the Home Economics Department). The last year she was listed as faculty is in the Fall of 1988.

[83] *Testimony* interview with Mrs. Waite, sold by Riplinger's A.V. Publications, Corp.

[84] Ibid.

[85] Divorce Record Case No. 84-CV-0652, *Gail Ludwig Kaleda v. Frank Kaleda*, August 6, 1984, including detailed Separation Agreement. On file at Portage County Common Pleas, Clerk of Courts, P.O. Box 1035, Ravenna, OH 44266, http://www.co.portage.oh.us/clerkofcourts.htm, http://www.portageco.com/misc_countyrecords.htm.

to Gail, she pursued the divorce anyway, which became final on August 6, 1984.[86] On that same day, Mr. Kaleda was made to file a Quit Claim Deed, prepared by Gail's attorney, to relinquish the house over to Gail.[87] Then, moving right along, on September 4, **less than one month after the divorce became final, Gail and Michael applied for a marriage license** at the Summit County Probate Court.[88] At the end of September, Gail conveyed the house to new owners via Warranty Deed.[89] Then just ten days after that, on October 9, she and Michael, not yet married, obtained a Warranty Deed with the Botnick Building Company, Inc. for a condominium being built in the Village of Munroe Falls, Summit County, Ohio.[90] Although not yet married, they were listed as "husband and wife" on the deed. As it appears, Gail had set her plans in motion ahead of time, on the day she filed for the divorce.

---

[86] Ibid. Is there any wonder that Gail told her husband's attorney, "It's none of your business," when he asked her if she was in agreement with Mr. Kaleda about working on their marriage and staying together? She somehow got Mr. Kaleda to recant his counterclaim against her and once he did, the divorce went to trial, and was finalized 14 days later, in Gail's favor.

[87] Quit Claim Deed, Vol. 1018, P. 204, September 26, 1984, prepared by Gail's attorney. On file at the Portage County, Ohio, Recorder's Office.

[88] Pre-Marital Certificate No. 59311, Marriage License Application, September 4, 1984, on file at the Summit County Probate Court, 209 S. High Street, Akron, Ohio 44308,
http://www.cpclerk.co.summit.oh.us/publicRecReq.asp.

[89] Warranty Deed Joint and Survivor Form, Vol. 1018, P.0297, September 28, 1984, prepared by Gail's attorney; on file at the Portage County, Ohio, Recorder's Office. The document indicates that Gail Riplinger was planning on transferring the house and property before the divorce was finalized, as the first transfer stamp states July 28, 1984, with the final transfer recorded as September 28, 1984.

[90] Warranty Deed 189738, Vol. 6995, P. 577-79, Botnick Building Company, Inc., listed as Grantor with Michael D. Riplinger and Gail A. Ludwig Riplinger, husband and wife, listed as Grantee, dated October 9, 1984 (18 days before they married). The fact that they had themselves listed as "husband and wife" when they were not yet married indicates that they had been planning ahead of time to get married.

A municipal judge wed Gail and Michael on October 27, 1984—**just two months after her second divorce became final.**[91] Continuing in their seemingly hurried fashion, the newlyweds signed a Survivorship Deed on March 26, 1984[92] and moved into their new condo. Their daughter, Bryn, was born three years later.[93] In 1994, the Riplinger's sold the condo[94] and relocated to the countryside of Ararat, Virginia, where they operate A.V. Publications from their home.[95]

During a lecture at a 1995 pastors' conference (at which Michael and their young daughter were present) after telling the audience falsely that she had no husband while a professor at KSU, she said:

> **When I met my husband** [Michael], for **our first date**, I said, "They're having a meeting at the Catholic Church...We

---

[91] Marriage record No. 59311, Michael Dominick Riplinger and Gail Anne Ludwig, October 27, 1984, Summit County, Ohio. The couple were married by William B. Pike, municipal judge of Cuyahoga Falls, Ohio. On file at the Summit County Probate Court, 209 S. High Street, Akron, OH 44308 http://www.cpclerk.co.summit.oh.us/ publicRecReq.asp.
[92] Estate by the Entireties with Survivorship Deed, 202899, Vol. 7037, P. 501, March 26, 1985, prepared by Michael D. Riplinger. Interestingly, the couple implemented a "release all rights of dower in the above described premises."
[93] Birth certificate for Bryn Ayn Riplinger.
[94] Survivorship Deed and transfer of property, August 31, 1994, on file with the Summit County Recorder, OH.
[95] A.V. Publications, Corp. has been registered in Gail and Michael Riplinger's names (and more recently Bryn's, also) with the Commonwealth of Virginia, SCC I.D. No. F1193913, since 3/13/1995 when it was transferred from Ohio: http://scc-internet.scc.virginia.gov/corporate/ arfilings/corpfilings.asp?charternumber=f1193913. Gail lists herself as President/Treasurer, daughter Bryn as Vice-President, and Michael as Secretary. The address of A.V. Publications, Corp. is registered as that of the Riplingers' home. A.V. Publications is listed in Virginia business guides under the Riplinger home address.

have to go pass out tracts, you know." So, that was our first date, going to pass out tracts at the Catholic Church. [96]

Now that the truth is known, does Riplinger actually expect people to believe that for her first date with her current husband that she was a dutiful Christian desiring to pass out tracts at a Catholic Church meeting? **Was she a dutiful Christian wife as she abandoned her husband while dating and then marrying another?** She failed to tell the congregation about this, **covering the truth even then**. Something about her story does not smell very good. To reiterate the truth: she has lied, several times over, and all those to whom she has lied deserve an explanation and an apology. And what about Mr. Riplinger, the man at the center of this controversy? What kind of leader is he? What kind of man? We can either side with what the Bible says, in context, or we can disobey it for our own convenience and be hypocrites.

God says the "virtuous woman" does her husband "good and not evil all the days of her life." She does not abandon him for another man. Does Riplinger disdain the NASB so much because in Proverbs 23:17 it calls this kind of woman "adulterous" instead of just "strange" (KJV)? How about the NIV, which minces no words when it calls the "strange woman" the "wayward wife"? Are some of these "new versions" too honest for someone with Gail Riplinger's lack of conscience? Is this possibly the real reason why she attacks and falsely accuses them? Divorce is evil! Why? It destroys homes, families, lives, and most of all the covenant of marriage ordained by God. God hates divorce as much as he hates anything else that destroys the sanctity of marriage—even as much as He hates homosexual marriage. A perversion of marriage is a perversion of marriage, period.

The real question is: in actuality, who "rejected" and "abandoned" whom? The second divorce record shows Mr. Kaleda

---

[96] *Testimony, Question & Answer*, pastors' conference, sold by A.V. Publications, Corp.

was currently unemployed and suffering from depression.[97] This was at the tail end of the 1980's recession, when some jobs were hard to come by and certain professions did not fare well. And, for all anyone knows, he was very possibly aware that his wife was seeing another man and planning to leave him. He had stated in his counterclaim that Gail had "not been a dutiful wife." Gail kicked him out of the home they shared, making him homeless until he was able to find temporary lodging.[98] The Lord has given no allowance for a person to divorce his or her spouse because of unemployment or depression—or for any other illness or economic status.[99]

Despite hard times for Mr. Kaleda, Gail's job remained stable throughout the recession, even when Kent State University was experiencing some financial cutbacks.[100] The divorce document states her assistant professor's salary at KSU was $20,000 a year—not bad for 1984—and that with their mortgage paid in full. For the first five years of their marriage, when Gail had been a full-time student, not yet employed, Mr. Kaleda was the primary support person. In fact, because Gail was a fulltime university student without a job before 1980, their leases at the trailer park and other temporary residences were in her husband's name, since he was the only one employed at the time. Once Gail became established as a well-paid university instructor, why did she not lend monetary and emotional support to her husband when she

---

[97] Divorce Record Case No. 84-CV-0652, *Gail Ludwig Kaleda v. Frank Kaleda*, August 6, 1984, including detailed Separation Agreement. On file at Portage County Common Pleas, Clerk of Courts, P.O. Box 1035, Ravenna, OH 44266, http://www.co.portage.oh.us/clerkofcourts.htm, http://www.portageco.com/misc_countyrecords.htm.
[98] Ibid.
[99] Matthew 19:9: "And I say unto you, Whosoever shall put away his wife, **except it be for fornication, and shall marry another, committeth adultery**: and whoso marrieth her which is put away doth commit adultery." This rule applies to the wife as much as to the husband. They are "one flesh" (Matthew 19:6) and God hates divorce (Malachi 2:16).
[100] Kent State University archive records from the early 1980s, during the presidency of Michael Schwartz, indicate financial cutbacks and a freeze on the hiring of faculty.

had the ability to do so, instead of divorcing him during such a difficult time in his life? What about the wedding vows that declare "in sickness and in health" and "for richer or for poorer"? Instead of being the helpmeet a wife should be, she abandoned her husband and quickly married another man. No matter how hard it might be for some to accept it, sadly, that's the dirty truth. The controversial circumstances surrounding her second divorce are most likely why Gail Riplinger didn't want anyone to know much about her past during the 1990s, as she built a name and a bank account for herself.

It has been said that God did not create marriage entirely to make mankind happy but to teach mankind how to be holy. Through marrying an imperfect person, both spouses learn to depend on God, to submit to Him and to obey His commands, to submit to one another, how to forgive and love one another more, and to learn the essence of the core of the gospel of the Lord Jesus Christ and the mystery of the Bride of Christ and His love for her. Divorce is never an option unless adultery has occurred and the guilty spouse refuses to stop and then work to repair the marriage. Considering the overwhelming evidence, the wayward spouse in this case was Gail Anne Ludwig Latessa Kaleda Riplinger.

If Riplinger were truly the innocent party in her divorces, she would have been honest and open about them from the start, with nothing to hide, rather than shrouding her past in secrecy and lies.

Instead of taking responsibility for her divorces and lies, Riplinger has channeled her angry energy into writing a 61-paged diatribe[101] against those who dared to tell the Church what she was

---

[101] This latest attack launched at her "critics" is titled *Traitors*. It contains much false information about the 13 people whom she has labeled "traitors," as pointed out in Dr. D.A. Waites rebuttal *A Warning on Gail Riplinger's KJB & Multiple Inspiration Heresy* (2010, The Bible for Today, Collingswood, NJ). Riplinger plays fast and loose with scripture, spewing as many verses as possible, out of context, at her targets, making herself appear righteous and her "critics" as the devil. The attack followed the heels of the exposure of her unbiblical divorces. She found the time to write a 61-paged polemic but not a letter of apology to those to whom she lied.

hiding. In this latest saint-singeing tirade—which matches the fervor of *KJV Ditches Blind Guides* from a decade ago—she unloads both barrels on every person with whom she holds a grudge—dead and alive—labeling them as "traitors," while never mentioning one word about her divorces or why she lied about them and falsely accused her first two husbands to her daughter. If there is one thing that Gail Riplinger has proved herself proficient at, it is stabbing others vengefully with her pen. If she were to put as much energy into being honest, and into apology and truth, as she does into attacking the opponents she creates for herself, there would be no need for such a heated altercation. She is able to focus her time and attention on writing a 61-paged invective, yet totally ignore her public sin. In the end, it will be herself she hurts the most as she burns down her bridges.

Those sickeningly sudsy soap operas and sleazy celebrity lives

Most people are probably aware of how Hollywood mocks the God-ordained design for marriage and family. Men are never "right" and no matter how good or valiant they try to be, it's never good enough. Women are often portrayed as being "better" and "smarter" than men, independent and correct, no matter what. Sexually immoral filth of all kinds is spewed across the screen. Celebrities divorce one spouse and move on to another, without a care for the solemnity of wedding vows.[102] Soap operas glorify a person leaving his or her spouse to go on to the next, and then to the next, and on and on—slimy, sickening, sexually immoral disobedience in the face of God—people making

---

[102] Just a few examples would be: Madonna (married twice; unfaithful to the second husband), Mel Gibson (divorced his wife for a younger woman with whom he had a baby out of wedlock, and then separated), Elizabeth Taylor (eight or nine husbands), Robin Williams (unfaithful to his first wife, married several times), and the list goes on.

themselves one with more than one person, without care for the consequences, totally against God's design.

Celebrities don't care much for heeding God's commands, and, sadly, neither do a lot of their fans. Recently, popular actor Mel Gibson divorced his wife of nearly 30 years and began cohabitating up with a woman whom he had impregnated while still married. Did this affect the loyal support of the majority of his fans? Did they express outrage or expect him to answer for his wrong? Did they decide to boycott his films as a way to show their disapproval of his moral laxity? For most of them, NO. When he came on stage at the Golden Globe Awards, January 17, 2010, the audience cheered wildly for him.[103] His latest films are selling out at the theaters. The world accepts a code that says, "It doesn't matter what my favorite celebrities are doing in their private lives. Their private lives are not my business. I just care how they do their job of entertaining me." Romans 1:32 refutes that line of thinking. Yet, sadly, it is not much different for those who follow and defend Gail Riplinger despite that most of them now know the unscriptural nature of her two divorces, third marriage, and her lying about them. Like Mel Gibson's fans, some have said, "Her teaching is what's important. Her private life doesn't matter."[104] Really? God's word contradicts that line of thinking. If a person is practicing willful sin, his teaching is in vain. How did Paul instruct Timothy in the Lord?

> ...be thou an example of the believers, **in word**, **in conversation** [manner of living and personal conduct, morality], in charity, in spirit, in faith, **in purity** [concerning truth, etc.] (1 Timothy 4:12).

And what did Peter say?

---

[103] We do not watch celebrity award shows, or the like, but happened to see a recap of Mel Gibson receiving his award on the evening news.

[104] We have read comments such as this on public Internet bulletin boards. Of these comments, Paul might said, "I say this to your shame."

> ...what manner of persons ought ye to be **in all holy conversation** [pure, obedience in manner of living] **and godliness** (2 Peter 3:11).

Paul explained:

> But **I keep under my body** [subject one's self self-discipline, keep one's self in obedience to God], and **bring it into subjection** [under control]: lest that by any means, when I have preached to others, I myself should be a castaway (1 Corinthians 9:27).

When it's set forth in the word of God, it's meant for every Christian, not just everyone except Gail Riplinger. Yet, for some, when such immorality happens in the church with a favored author or teacher, they are slower to call it what it is than when the world does it. To this the Apostle Paul would say: "I speak this to your shame (1 Cor. 15:34)." We want our Presidents and other elected officials to have integrity and honesty, and to lead moral lives, but what about those who lead and teach in the body of Christ? What about those whose teaching we accept? Some Christians seem to think it's permissible to condemn the already condemned world while accepting impure and dishonest behavior in those they look up to. The severity of the sin depends on who's doing the sinning. Do we see the hypocrisy here? If we don't, we're in need of some prayerful soul-searching. Whether it is one unscriptural remarriage or a dozen, it doesn't matter. God's view on divorce is clear in scripture. In actuality, His rules are stricter for Christians than for the unsaved, because His children are supposed to know better.

God says:

> These things also belong to the wise. It is not good to have respect of persons in judgment. He that saith unto the wicked, Thou art righteous; him shall the people curse, nations shall abhor him: But to them that rebuke him shall be delight, and a good blessing shall come upon them (Proverbs 24:23-25).

Professing Christians (both pastors and lay persons) are making excuses for Mrs. Riplinger's divorces and lies (and *they* know who they are), allowing her to continue as if she's done nothing wrong. It is time for that to come to a stop. The unscriptural nature of her divorces and her lying about them doesn't matter to some, as if God gave them place to change His rules. If they continue in this line of thinking, one day they will have to take this up with God. They preach against divorce in their churches but defend her because they've piggybacked their cause for the KJV upon her teachings and she is "one of their own." Then there are those pastors who have long supported Riplinger who are remaining silent rather than addressing the issue. There's this hypocrisy: let's preach against divorce and gay marriage in our churches but when we find out that someone to whom we've granted a high degree of special privilege is guilty of sexual immorality, let's act as if it is no big deal. She lived in adultery against her second husband for 15 years after divorcing him, until he died in 1999, while a professing Christian, and while she was most active writing her books and teaching in church pulpits where few had the benefit of knowing. Her first husband is still living, nearly 40 years after the divorce.

Defining *Divorce* According to God's Standard

We are not talking about divorce where the reason is the only one allowed by the Lord, as stated in Matthew 19:9. There are innocent parties in some divorces and, sadly, many brothers and sisters in the Lord have experienced this human tragedy *against their will*, when their spouses (even those professing Christ) abandoned the marriage for one reason or another. There are women who have been left with young children when their husband decided to walk out, and men abandoned by wives who decided they no longer loved their husbands. We are talking about divorce where a person decides that for a reason other than their spouse has committed adultery and refused reconciliation he or she wants a divorce. The kind where a person meets someone else or decides they are no longer in love with their spouse (if they ever were). There are far too many divorces happening in America[105] where a spouse gets "bored" or finds another person who lights their fire. Today, marriage is a disposable commodity where divorce is taken lightly. One can throw away, or trade in, one's spouse for another like buying the next automobile or pair of shoes. People casually marry, thinking the consequences aren't all that serious, because divorce has become a back door way out when things stop going their way. Top surveys show that *professing* Christians, especially Baptists, make up a large portion of this American tragedy.[106] There's a serious problem within the fold, and it can only be remedied through repentance in each responsible heart and the local assembly. And many pastors need to get involved.

Not like Jael or Deborah

Now that we've identified predominant aspects of Gail Riplinger's life, we can see that she has falsely likened herself to these strongly obedient women of the Bible. Keeping the law of God, would Jael or

---

[105] Divorce Statistics Collection: http://www.divorcereform.org/stats.html and Divorce Reform Page: http://patriot.net/~crouch/divorce.html. In Moscow, Russia, snoring has been the cause of some divorce: http://www.divorcereform.org/ cau.html, but Russia is a godless nation. Other reported reasons for divorce are Internet relationships, money, and boredom (sexual and otherwise) with one's spouse. Of course, God approves of none of these. Time magazine addressed the divorce problem, September 17, 1999, with the article "Positive Illusions: From 'I do' to the Seven-Year Itch, a new study shows that marriage (surprise) is hard work," by Amy Dickinson: http://www.divorcereform.org/mel/aqualityofmarr.html. In November 2009, Dr. Phil reported the divorce rate in America at around 60%. America has an epidemic.

[106] Some polls indicate that divorce among Baptists is more prevalent than among "devout" Catholics. See Baptist polls at http://www.sullivan-county.com/bush/divorce.htm and http://www.baptiststandard.com/2000/1_12/pages/divorce.html.

Deborah have ignored 1 Peter 3:1-2, Ephesians 5:22-24, Colossians 3:18, or 1 Corinthians 14:34, which are built upon the law of God?

> Likewise, ye wives, **be in subjection to your own husbands**; that, if any obey not the word [are disobedient or unbelievers], they also may without the word be won by the conversation [Godly manner of life] of the wives; While they behold your chaste conversation [manner of living] coupled with fear [reverence for her husband].

> Wives, submit yourselves unto your own husbands, as unto the Lord. For the husband is the head of the wife, even as Christ is the head of the church: and he is the saviour of the body. Therefore as the church is subject unto Christ, so let the wives be to their own husbands in every thing.
> Wives, submit yourselves unto your own husbands, as it is fit [your duty] in the Lord.

> Let your women keep silence in the churches: for **it is not permitted unto them to speak**; but they are commanded to be under obedience, as also **saith the law**.

Because Jael and Deborah lived in obedience to God's word, they were commended—the evidence being that their God-fearing examples are preserved forever in scripture. They were each married to *one* husband. Scripture doesn't tell us whether these husbands were believers. Deborah and Jael recognized that men are leaders appointed by God, and they respected the men around them (including their husbands), even when those men where not fulfilling their leadership roles to the fullest. They didn't twist scripture out of context or misapply it for their own purposes. And they did not make lies their refuge (Isa. 28:15).

* * *

Nowhere does Scripture allow lying in order to defend the Bible or to glorify God. Yet, some seem to believe it is acceptable for Gail Riplinger to lie in her books and about herself in order to defend their mutual cause concerning the King James Version. In other words, she has been granted a free pass by some, simply because she is *in their camp*.[107] But God doesn't agree, as Romans 3:7-8 shows. The updated English of the NKJV makes these verses clearer:

> For if the truth of God has increased through my lie to His glory, [then] why am I also still judged a sinner? And why not say, "Let us do evil that good may come"? – as we are slanderously reported and as some affirm that we say. Their condemnation is just.

As scripture makes it clear, willful sin (the habitual practice of sin) can never bring glory to God. Lying to defend the word of God is actually disobedience against the word. In other words, when it comes to serving the God of the Bible, the end does not justify disobedient

---

[107] Despite Gail Riplinger's divorces and her lying about them to the Waites, and everyone at their January 2008 Princeton Bible Conference, becoming public information, pastors such Jeff Fugate of Clays Mill Road Baptist Church have *divisively* invited her to speak to their congregations concerning the Bible. Fugate, as host pastor, invited her as a guest speaker at the October 5-7, 2009, 38th National Bus Convention. According to the convention's flyer: "Dr. Gail Riplinger will be answering several crucial and timely questions concerning the KJB." (Flyer on file) Audio files for the 2009 convention, on her son-in-law Stephen Shutt's Berean Baptist (WPIP Radio, Winston-Salem, NC) web site, show Riplinger spoke there. It's unfortunate that the "timely questions" had nothing to do with Mrs. Riplinger's habit of lying about her past unscriptural divorces and other conflictual information. If anyone thinks Mrs. Riplinger is not *teaching doctrine*—especially to/over men—during these church events, they are deluding themselves and are in disobedience to scripture. There is an awkward silence within the King James Bible camp among the pastors and teachers who have endorsed Riplinger and her teachings over the past 17 years, when these people should be calling on her to take responsibility for her deceit and apologize to the people from whom she gained trust through her falsehood. The next thing that people need to do is thoroughly check the integrity of this woman's teachings.

means. God holds strong views about willful lying and those who make a habit of it:

> He that worketh deceit shall not dwell within my house: he that telleth lies shall not tarry in my sight (Psalm 101:7).
>
> Thou hast trodden down all them that err from thy statutes: for their deceit is falsehood (Psalm 119:118).
> Lying lips are abomination to the LORD: but they that deal truly are his delight (Proverbs 12:22).
>
> He that speaketh truth sheweth forth righteousness: but a false witness deceit (Proverbs 12:17).
>
> Deceit is in the heart of them that imagine evil... (Proverbs 12:20a).
> A poor man is better than a liar (Proverbs 19:22b).
>
> Do not bear false witness (Mark 10:19b).
>
> Wherefore putting away lying, speak every man truth with his neighbour: for we are members of one another (Ephesians 4:25).

While Christians can still sin, and do, a born-again person cares that he or she has sinned because he or she has a new nature and mind. Such a person no longer enjoys sin like they once did, because salvation is a supernatural transformation of the heart, mind, and soul. There is a change of attitude toward sinning. God's child doesn't continue in a willful disregard for his commands for too long before responding to the Holy Spirit's conviction and confessing his or her sin to God (1 John 1:9). The difference between the unregenerate (unsaved) person and the regenerate person is that the unregenerate doesn't care that his or her sin offends God, while the regenerate person is conscious of his or her sin and how God feels about it. The regenerate person no longer says, "I have done nothing wrong" after committing willful sin. Such a denial is a thing of the past. While the born-again person is not perfect and can still fall from time to time—still living in the corruptible body of flesh—he or she will desire repentance over willful sin, and he or she will seek to live his or her life in a manner pleasing to God and in obedience to His commands. That is one of the many miracles of the new nature. The Holy Spirit transforms a person. He or she is now aware of sin in a way they formerly were not. He or she will have a stronger desire to correct the problem and make it right with God instead of continually denying they are wrong. If there is no genuine difference between the deeds of a confessing Christian and those of an unsaved person, something is wrong and it should be a cause for concern.

> Therefore if any man be in Christ, he is a new creature: old things are passed away; behold, all things are become new (2 Corinthians 5:17).
>
> That ye put off concerning the former conversation the old man, which is corrupt according to the deceitful lusts; And be renewed in the spirit of your mind; and that ye put on the new man, which after God is created in righteousness and true holiness (Ephesians 4:22-24).
>
> All unrighteousness is sin... (1 John 5:17).
> If we say that we have no sin, we deceive ourselves, and the truth is not in us...If we say that we have not sinned, we make him a liar, and his word is not in us (1 John 1:8, 10).
>
> And hereby we do know that we know him, if we keep his commandments...He that saith, I know him, and keepeth not his commandments, is a liar, and the truth is not in him (1 John 2:3-4).

What person, after he or she has been saved from the gutter and adopted by a king, given new clothes, new shoes, good food to eat, and a new name desires to run back to the gutter and crawl around there?

Such a person would not do it for too long. When the King of kings has saved a person, and given him a place at His table, why would he wish to go back and live like a child of the wicked and destitute? Is that how one is to thank the One who gave *all* for the sake of the perishing? Does one desire to love and serve the good Master or turn on Him and disobey Him as if He does not see? Does the new nature not conquer the old and give victory, strength, and obedience to the believer? The Christian who is living in willful, habitual sin is out of fellowship with the Father, and if that person does not think so, he is fooling himself. A saved person will not stay too long in habitual sin. Even the prodigal son figured it out after a short season.

King David, one of God's redeemed, exhibited a sincere repentant heart, many times over, and did not cover or deny his sin for very long before confessing it. In Psalm 119:29 his desire is forever recorded: "Remove from me the way of lying..." This should be the desire of every true born-again child's heart. The "way of lying" (the habitual, ongoing practice) belongs to those who don't know God, as scripture indicates in many places.

We are not saying true born-again people don't sin after they are saved. 1 John makes it clear that a Christian can still sin but also that those who practice sin willfully, or as if they have no conscience about it, deceive themselves. It is habitual, willful, unrepentant lying we are addressing here.

> If we say that we have fellowship with him, and walk in darkness, we lie, and do not the truth (1 John 1:6).

Lying, as if without conscience or care, shouldn't be an ongoing practice of the person who professes to *know* to the Lord. And God's people should not give an ear to those who live that way. There are those who "lovest...lying rather than to speak righteousness (Psalm 52:3)," because such have never come to Christ and are in need of redemption. Jesus said He gives his children "the Spirit of truth (John 14:17)," and also, "If ye love me, keep my commandments (John

14:15)." When a professing Christian is found to be a consistent liar—even lying about past, serious sin—something is wrong. Where the Spirit of truth is missing, there should be concern. The same warning God gave to Israel still stands today:

> Repent, and turn yourselves from all your transgressions; so iniquity shall not be your ruin (Ezekiel 18:30b).

When a professing Christian is found sinning (lying, adultery, etc.), scripture instructs:

> Brethren, if any of you do err from the truth, and one convert him; Let him know, that he which converteth the sinner from the error of his way shall save a soul from death, and shall hide a multitude of sins (James 5:19-20).

This cannot be accomplished while Christians deny the sin of one of their own. If Gail Riplinger's supporters let her continue in her lying, how can she be helped? How will she realize her need for repentance? They're doing her a serious disfavor.

> **Blessed** is that man that maketh the LORD his trust, and respecteth not the proud, **nor such as turn aside to lies** (Psalm 40:4).

A Recap

It should be obvious that Riplinger hid the sin of her divorces from God's people, and most likely because she knew that *they knew* they were not according to scripture and that God's people would have most likely not given her the audience she obtained by hiding them. Instead of being honest, she chose to cover the truth unrighteously and make her life a lie. When the divorces were finally discovered and she was asked about them, she lied to continue to hide them and protect herself. She has also lied about (slandered) her first two husbands (through her daughter) to make them look *bad*, so that her divorces would appear justified. Does she care about all those people whose money she took in book and video sales? They trusted her to be an upstanding, honest, person of integrity and family values.

Gail Riplinger Lies

There is no nicer way to say it: Gail Riplinger has lied and continues to deny doing wrong. Dr. and Mrs. Waite trusted her when, as concerned Christian brethren, they wanted to know if the news of her divorces was true. Not because they are gossips, not because they like to meddle in people's lives, but because they wanted to make sure that she was not guilty of the sin of which they had heard. She lied to them when she told them that her current husband is the only man to whom she has ever been married, and they trusted her because they had every reason to trust her. She lied to Mrs. Waite in a 1995 interview, and to the pastors at the conference, when she said she had no husband before she met Michael Riplinger. She has lied in *New Age Bible Versions*, concerning other Bible versions. She has *lied*, chosen deception over truth, and therein lies the brunt of the problem. Her refusal to tell the truth indicates a lack of repentance—both for the sinful nature of her divorces and for her lying about them. Riplinger does herself more damage by refusing to acknowledge the problem and repent. Why is it that she will not acknowledge her wrong?

During the *Action 60s* interview, in 1994, Riplinger told the hosts:

> The way we get saved, we have to have **a humble heart**. We have to **admit that we're wrong**.

Gail Riplinger needs to live up to her words and return to a humble heart. She needs to admit that she has done wrong in covering the truth and continuing to lie to God's people.

Who is Gail Riplinger?
Part Two

Contradictions Abound

"Things that are different are not the same."[1]
 – Dr. Mickey Carter, Landmark Baptist Church

Wherefore putting away lying,
speak every man truth with his neighbour:
for we are members one of another. – Ephesians 4:25

It is important to verify whether someone is telling the truth about him or herself, because if a person is not being honest about whom he or she is, how can he or she be trusted with anything else he or she says? Let us deal seriously with the subject of dishonesty because it is the primary reason this booklet needed to be written. Riplinger's willful dishonesty concerning her divorces goes hand in hand with the multitude of intentional misrepresentations found in her books and misinformation she has given about herself.

In an interview, Riplinger stated:

---

[1] Mickey Carter, *Things That Are Different Are Not the Same: The Truth About the Battle for the Preserved King James Bible,* Landmark Baptist Press, 1993, as advertised at Voice From the Pews, Ludowici, GA: http://www.voicefromthepews.com/page.cfm?id=75.]

> You know, truth is independent of who is saying it. If something is the truth, then we need to evaluate the information rather than looking at the person... [2]

As demonstrated in chapter one, Gail Riplinger has few qualms about lying when it suits her. While truth is independent of who presents it, when a person is found lying and that person is a teacher trusted by the Church, we must start "looking at the person." While truth is independent and absolute, lies are dependent on the sinful will. People are responsible for their actions.

Riplinger has lied about people and Bible history, has misrepresented facts and the words of others for her gain, and she has even taken scripture out of context to make it support her means. She has fabricated information and raised a false report, accusing people and modern English versions of saying what they do not say. Just because some people do not wish to believe this, it does not make it any less true. People have brought these problems to her attention, yet she has refused to address them. She has even gone on uncharitable attacks, slanderously mocking and vilifying other people in an un-Christ-like manner.[3] Rather than exhibiting repentance, she has expressed continual denial of her errors and an attitude of "I have done nothing wrong." The dishonesty has continued with each book—with the distortions of earlier books rehashed in later ones.

In this chapter, some of her major contradictions and false information about herself will be examined.

---

[2] *Actions Sixties*, with Herman and Sharron Bailey, P.O. Box 6922, Clearwater, Florida, 34618, ©1994. Riplinger's A.V. Publications, Corp. sells this interview series.
[3] This is evidenced throughout the booklets titled *G.A. Riplinger Exposes Critics of KJV, King James Version Ditches Blind Guides* (c. 1994) and *Traitors* (2010), both published by Riplinger's A.V. Publications, Corp.

Would the *real* salvation testimony please stand up?

During the 1990s Gail Riplinger had what appeared to be a sure testimony, which she shared during many of her church lectures. She would tell pretty much the same account, most of the time including the same age at which she was saved: 26 (see Chapter One, p. 6). However, contradictions exist in the timing and different ages she has stated:

> I received the Lord Jesus Christ as my Savior when **I was twenty-six years old**, and **I was in graduate school**.[4]

> I was saved [at Kent State University] **as a graduate student**...[5]

> **I was a graduate school student** at Kent State University and **I was not saved** ... And I receive the Lord Jesus Christ as my Savior **in my late 20s**.[6]

There are several contradictions here and at the time she gave these lectures, most of her supporters knew nothing about her other than what she told them. First, when Gail Riplinger was in her "late 20s," she was actually **not** a "graduate student" at any university. Kent State University records show she did not enter graduate school until she was 31 years of age, in late 1978. She graduated with her

---

[4] Lecture at Berean Baptist Church, first visit, sold on DVD by Riplinger as *Riplinger Lecture Series: Overview, Sword Slays the Dragon, King James Bible Perfection or NIV, NKJV, NASV Perversion*, A.V. Publications, Corp.
[5] Lecture at Temple Baptist Church, Knoxville, TN, 1996, sold on DVD by Riplinger as *Research Update, Q & A, King James Bible Perfection or NIV, NKJV, NASV, Perversions*. In this series, she spoke during the Sunday school hour, Sunday morning service, and Sunday evening service.
[6] *Riplinger Testimony with Questions & Answers*, lecture and interview (with Yvonne Waite), recorded at a pastors' conference, sold by Riplinger's A.V. Publications, Corp.

undergraduate degree, a B.A. in Interior Design, in June of 1978. The last time we checked, the age of 31 is not considered one's "late twenties." She was also not in graduate school yet when she was 26; she was in the middle of working on her undergraduate degree. It appears Riplinger is having a difficult time remembering.

In 2005, when we began our research into Riplinger's material, we wrote to her company, A.V. Publications to kindly ask where we could read her Christian testimony, since her web site's biographical page contained her professional credentials but nothing of a personal spiritual nature. At that time, we gave her the benefit of any doubt. Here is the curt, anonymous reply we received:

> Riplinger's testimony is available on audiotape or CD (Call us at 1-800-435-4535).[7]

So, instead of being directed to a place where one should be able to simply read her testimony, we were offered a product that we could purchase.[7] It would seem that a Christian's testimony would be given free of charge. Does not scripture instruct us to be ready to give an answer for the hope we have? A little while later, several people gave us a collection of her lectures on DVD and we became familiar with the contradictory statements in her testimony.

As mentioned in Chapter One, the age she stated most often was the age of 26. However, after her divorces were publicized, she seemed to hold to her "late 20s."[8] Does "late 20s" include the age of 26

---

[7] According to Riplinger's A.V. Publications, Corp., catalog, the audio CD version is sold for $10.00 and the video DVD version $14.95, a pretty price to pay just to hear someone's Christian testimony.
[8] In a radio interview with Riplinger, November 19, 2009, on WBLW radio (Grace Baptist Church, Gaylord, MI), "The Rise & Shine Time," when asked to share her salvation testimony, she said: "I was raised a Roman Catholic ... But it's been over 30 years now [before 1979] since some dear soul-winner, like you have at your church, challenged me to read the New Testament." When one of the hosts asked her how old she was when she was saved, she answered: "I was in my late 20s. Um, about 29 years old." Riplinger has said many times that she was in graduate school when she was saved, yet

WHO IS GAIL RIPLINGER? | 73

in Gail Riplinger's mind? Or is she actually not certain when one of the largest events in life took place? While most people might not remember the exact day or year, most are within the ballpark. It seems odd that she would forget, especially when she can view her own lecture videos to refresh her memory.[9] If she is not certain of her salvation testimony, how can anyone else be? There is so much contradiction, even in something so fundamentally important.

Riplinger and her daughter cannot seem to concur on which scripture passage is the one that prompted Riplinger to be saved. Riplinger has stated at different times, in various places, that the verse "Ye are of your father the devil" is what led her to become saved.[10] Yet, her daughter stated in her 2009 tribute to her parents' 25th anniversary: "[the past events of her life] left her ripe for the verse where Jesus said He had come 'to heal the brokenhearted.' This verse led her to Christ..." The themes of these two verses are very different. Did her daughter not verify this information with her mother, to be sure that it was accurate, or is she not aware of the verse her mother has mentioned many times in the past? Beside her age at salvation, has Riplinger forgotten which verse it was that led her to Christ?

"Bedridden" for six years, or not?

Another concern is her repeated claim, mentioned in several lecture videos, interviews, and writings, that "God" gave her a "disability" in the form of an always unnamed "connective tissue disease," which made her "bedridden" with extreme pain and immobility for "six years," so that she could "collate" Bible versions and write *New Age*

---

according to KSU records she did not begin graduate school until she was 31, in late 1978.

[9] Each video cited in this chapter is sold by Riplinger in her A.V. Publications, Corp. catalog, available at her web site.

[10] WBLW radio, "The Rise & Shine Time," interview, op. cit. She has stated this in some other interviews, as well.

Bible Versions. According to the dictionary, *bedridden* means "confined to one's bed by illness, injury, or weakness."[11] She has said this "disability" required her "retirement"[12] from her job as a professor at Kent State University. While in some lectures and interviews she mentioned the "disability," in others she left it out.

Bedridden yet Able to Go to the Bookstore and Library

In *New Age Bible Versions*, she completely leaves out any hint of a disability and even gives a contradictory account of the six years:

Page 1:

> Much digging **in libraries** and manuscripts from around the world..."

Page 45:

> Overheard on **one of my infrequent research visits to the local New Age bookstore** was the comment by the owner to a customer selecting a book, "I don't know if you are ready for that; you'd better start with something that doesn't shock a beginner."

Page 440:

> Their [J.B. Phillips' translations of the "bible" (sic)] widespread distribution was evident **on today's visit to the**

---

[11] *Webster's Third New International Dictionary of the English Language*, Unabridged, Merriam-Webster Inc., Publishers, Springfield, MA.

[12] Gail Riplinger with Noah Hutchings, *Which Bible is God's Word?*, 1994, Hearthstone Publishing, Ltd., Oklahoma City, p. 6. Riplinger's quote: "I have done a six-year-long, laborious, word-for-word collation of [the new translations]. This was made possible because of my disability retirement from the university."

Kent State University bookstore which housed a small stock of three bibles for sale, *one King James Version* and *two* Phillip's translations. [Italics in original]

While she was "bedridden," she somehow managed to go to the local New Age bookstore and to the Kent State bookstore. How is that? Did she take her bed with her? In the late 1980s and early 1990s, in order to look at "manuscripts from around the world," one would have had to hop a plane for London, Switzerland, etc. It has to be asked: How does one obtain these manuscripts when one is confined to one's bed ("bedfast") for six years? No manuscript archive, such as the John Rylands Library (United Kingdom), the Chester Beatty Library (Dublin, Ireland), or the Bibliotheca Bodmeriana (Cologny, Switzerland), is going to privately send their fragile, ancient manuscripts to an unknown university professor in Ohio. Today, many of these libraries have their collections available for viewing online. However, during the six years that Riplinger claims she did her research, there was no Internet as we know it today.

The Story Changes

Not long after *New Age Bible Versions* was published, Riplinger began speaking in churches and giving interviews. This is when she began claiming that "God" gave her a "disability" and she became bedridden, so that she could do full-time research:
To the congregation of Berean Baptist Church, Winston-Salem, NC:

> I told the Lord, I said, "Lord, it appears that there are some serious problems with these new Bible versions. If you would give me a chance to collate them word for word, so I can see how involved these changes are [sic]." And, so, he, ah—**I became disabled** and **I spent the next six years in bed**. **I**

> **couldn't walk**, I couldn't see very well, **I couldn't use my hands very well**, **I was very, very ill**, and I was **in a lot of pain**. And I thought the Lord had, had sort of—didn't quite answer my prayer the way I thought he would, because I thought maybe I'd sit at the beach somewhere and flip Bible pages or something. But he had a different idea. But **over the course of six years**, I collated every single word in the modern versions, comparing them with the King James Bible. …And, ah, the product of that six-year research is the book *New Age Bible Versions*.¹³

To the congregation of Temple Baptist Church, Knoxville, TN:

> I said to the Lord, "Give me a chance **to collate these versions**, so I can see exactly what's going on" … So, I asked the Lord that and **he gave me a disability**. So, **I spent the next six years in bed**—couldn't walk very well, couldn't see real well. Um, bad—my hands—**I couldn't grasp a pencil with my hands**. I developed what's called a connective tissue disease. So, **I spent six years in bed**. And that was his answer to my prayers. And the process of being **in bed six years in total, absolute pain**—I mean, beyond, you know, **50 on the Richter Scale** … and this thumb didn't work. … **I couldn't go to the library**, so I had to order things through interlibrary loan. … **I laid in bed for six years**…¹⁴

---

¹³ *Overview, King James Bible Perfection or NIV, NKJV, NASV Perversion*, lectures recorded at Berean Baptist Church, Winston-Salem, NC, Dr. Ron Baity, pastor; televised over WBFX and aired over WPIP radio. This set of lectures is produced and sold on DVDs by Riplinger via her company A.V. Publications, Corp.

¹⁴ *Research Update, Q & A Session, King James Bible Perfection or NIV, NKJV, NASV Perversion*, lectures recorded at Temple Baptist Church, 2100 W. Woodrow Dr., Knoxville, TN, and televised on the Scripps Howard cable network and WPMC-TV, 1996. This set of lectures is sold by Riplinger's

To the hosts of the television program *Action Sixties*:

> And I prayed to the Lord, and I said, "Lord, you know I love my students,"—at that time, **the Lord had not given me any children of my own**, and I loved these young people, and I said, "Lord, you know, I need to look into this. Let's—give me some time." And, so, ah, **I became disabled** [laughs]. **I went on a disability retirement**, and it was the Lord's blessing in disguise, and **I managed to lay in bed for about six years**. And **in the course of laying in bed for six years, collated word-for-word every single word in the new versions**, comparing each one. ... I have a connective tissue disease and, ah, that's what allowed me to do **a six-year collation** of new Bible versions. [15]

To Noah Hutchings of Southwest Radio Church:

> I have done a six-year-long, laborious, word-for-word collation of [the new translations]. This was made possible because of my **disability retirement** from the university. [16]

In some of these accounts, she mentioned not having any children when the disability began. Then, to the congregation of Gospel Light Baptist Church, Walkertown, NC, when telling them about the disability, she said:

> I said to the Lord, I said, "Lord, I love these students"—they were my children at that time, because **the Lord hadn't given me any children**—just the way the bus children are your children, sort of. And, I said, "Give me a chance to sit

---

A.V. Publications, Corp. Riplinger spoke these words in the first half of her lecture on the "new versions."
[15] *Action Sixties* broadcast, op. cit.
[16] Gail Riplinger with Noah Hutchings, *Which Bible is God's Word?*, 1994, Hearthstone Publishing, Ltd., Oklahoma City, p. 6.

down and collate these Bible versions," and He did that—**He gave me a disability**—and I became disabled. And **I was bedridden for six years, never left the house for six years, other than to go to the doctors**—or Cleveland Clinic—**couldn't move, really, couldn't turn over in bed, could hardly see, could hardly use my hands, could hardly walk**. My poor little girl—you know, **I had just had a little baby**, when I was forty, then—I'm now almost fifty. But I had a little baby then and poor little thing, she'd lay in bed, and my husband would have to put peanut butter sandwiches in the drawer and then she'd, you know, waddle in the room in time for lunch and she'd get the peanut butter sandwiches out of the drawer. So, it was a real, real difficult time. **But during that six-year period, I collated the new Bible versions word for word…It took about eight to twelve hours a day…** [17]

In this account, she started out telling them she had no children and had prayed to God for time to collate Bibles, to which He gave her a disability, and then she suddenly mentioned she'd just had a baby. What she did not specifically point out is that the supposed six years began around the same time that she had her daughter, in 1987.[18] She mentioned being 40 when her daughter was born; she turned 40 in 1987.[19] In this account of the story, it appears as if the disability started

---

[17] Sold by Riplinger in her A.V. Publications catalog as part of the Riplinger Lecture Series, *Detailed Update: King James Bible Perfection, New Versions Perversion* (Q & A with Pastors), recorded at Gospel Light Baptist Church, 890 Walkertown-Guthrie Rd., Walkertown, NC. (Riplinger occasionally changes the titles of her lectures.)

[18] Birth certificate of "Bryn Ayn Riplinger." Bryn's full name can be verified on the copyright page of Gail Riplinger's book *The Language of the King James Bible*, where "Bryn Ayn" is credited with "assistance in historical research."

[19] Birth certificate of Gail Anne Ludwig. Born October 1947, in Columbus, OH, to Wilson B. and Helen G. (Frech) Ludwig. On file with the Office of Vital Records, Columbus, OH.

before the birth of her daughter. Yet, in another lecture, she places the disability's start after her daughter's birth, as will be shown below.

In most of her lectures, did she leave out the mention of her daughter's birth coinciding with the disability because people might ask questions about how she managed to care for a very young child while completely bedridden? She never mentions the year that the so-called disability began or what year her daughter was born. It seems as if she does not want people to know *when* she left Kent State University (KSU), as this would cast questions upon her story and its varying contradictions.

According to KSU records, she did not leave employment until late 1988. In order to have a "six-year" disability and with *New Age Bible Versions* published in 1993 (six years following the birth of her daughter and time when she said she was disabled),[20] she would have had to leave KSU by early 1987. If she left KSU in late 1988, this means the disability and research period was closer to four years, not six. And by 1994, she appeared healthy and able-bodied as she began to give interviews and then two-hour lectures on her feet. This brings up the question: Was the real reason she left KSU due to a "disability retirement" or because she wanted to stay home with her daughter until she was old enough to enter school? If she wanted to stay home with her daughter, she is to be commended for that, since there is no job higher on earth for a woman. However, the question must then be asked: If she was completely incapacitated, in the way she stated, how was she able to care for her daughter? Her story holds unexplainable contradictions. Rearing a toddler is one of life's most challenging tasks. It is impossible to care for a helpless infant or rear a toddler while being confined to one's bed with a crippling disability.

In reality, "little babies"—even young toddlers—cannot eat peanut butter sandwiches until they have an ample set of teeth, know how to effectively chew and swallow, and no longer *choke* easily, which is usually between two and three years of age. Peanut butter is

---

[20] The printing date on the first printing of *New Age Bible Versions* is March 1993.

sticky and, for young children, not easy to swallow—especially when on bread. It is among the number one choking hazards for young children. No toddler should ever eat peanut butter sandwiches without an able-bodied adult closely supervising her. No young toddler should be left to help herself to peanut butter sandwiches left in a drawer when her mother cannot even care for herself. It is a toddler's nature to explore and get into things. She needs constant, responsible supervision to ensure her safety at all times.

Who took care of the daughter while she was a helpless infant in need of round-the-clock feedings, diapering, rocking, bathing, laundry, etc.? Who took care of her during her toddler years when she needed constant adult supervision, toilet training, care while ill, and proper nutrition? Does Riplinger expect people to believe that her toddler daughter just lay in bed all day, not walking and running around the home like normal children that age? Who took care of the disabled Gail Riplinger, who couldn't even turn herself in bed or walk, and who therefore was unable to cook, bathe, or barely feed herself with her non-working hands, at the same time that her daughter needed constant supervision and care? People who cannot turn themselves in bed require around-the-clock care; otherwise, they can develop painful bedsores and risk infection, blood clots, and pneumonia. If Riplinger claims her husband did all the care, then who went to work so that the bills were paid? If he was Gail and Bryn's main caregiver during this time, why did the daughter have to get her lunch out of a drawer?

The contradictions continue in this account of her "six-years" story, as told to a group of pastors at a conference:

> Well, two weeks before school started, I found out that I was going to have a baby ...and, um, I had something called placenta preva [sic], where the baby's upside down or backwards, or something, and you have to lay in bed for nine months. ... **I had the placenta preva** [sic], so **I got to stay in bed for nine months**, and so **I collated twelve hours a day for nine months** the New American Standard, word for word, comparing it with the King James Version. ... Since I was

pregnant and I don't think, you know, women should work who have children, I stayed home after this. So, God answered my prayers and I got to stay home and research the book. But to my surprise, **I developed a disease**—and it wasn't just a disease—something overtook me. **They called it "connective tissue disease" or "collagen disease," where I was completely bed-fast for six years**. And when I say bed-fast, I mean **I couldn't turn**—**I could hardly turn over**, all right? And **I couldn't use my thumbs**, I couldn't—my eyes were totally bloodshot, they were totally covered with blood, **I couldn't see very well**. And, so, **I had to keep my head under a pillow** and I could go—you know, **at night I could go out a little bit**—but our house is painted white and I couldn't really go in very many of the rooms—**I couldn't go out to the mailbox**, so, essentially for—**other than going to the doctor a few times, for about six years I was in the house**.

    I used to look out the window at the little old ladies and think, *Oh, if I could rake the leaves or if I could just get out of bed*. But what God did over that period of six years—and I, and I said to the Lord, I said, "Lord, you know, I quit my job to, to do this research for you. *Why* would you put me in such an incapacitated state where I can't do research?" And the Lord showed me, over a period of years, that it wasn't gonna be me and research and library, it was gonna be the Holy Spirit showing me things, and he was gonna take me aside, just like he did Ezekiel—Ezekiel was on one side for a year and on another side for a while, and he was dumb, and everything else. And **the Holy Spirit was gonna do the work and this was gonna be *his* book**, and **it wasn't gonna be my book** at some head, cognitive research-type thing. It was gonna be something that he was gonna do. ... And, essentially, what would happen I would lay in bed all day—not through laziness—I was, **I couldn't move**, I couldn't—**I was in so much pain**, it was just, ah, **it's on the 50 on the Richter Scale with pain**. And, so, ah, **I'd lay in bed all day and I'd be in so much pain**.

Well, when you lay in bed all day you can't sleep at night. And, so, he would, **he would say to me** at about ten o'clock at night, he'd say [laughs], he'd say, "Well, get up and work on the book," [laughs] and I'd say, "No, I'm too sick [laughs]." And he'd say, "Get up and work on the book," and I'd say, "No."—You see, we fought for 15 minutes every night for six years [laughs] and, ah, then after I told him I was too sick, he'd say, "You're in too much pain to sleep, aren't you?" and I said, "Yeah, I know," and, so, he said, "Well, get up and work on the book." And, so, I would always say, "I'm a woman and I don't think women should do this," [laughs] and he goes, "Get up and work on the book!" And, so, he goes, "Women make fine secretaries—that's all we need here [laughs]." So, um—but every night for six years we had this little fifteen-minute battle and **I'd get up and I'd work on it**, and **I would sit there in that chair**, for six years. And I don't know if you've ever been on a rollercoaster but you know how white your knuckles are when you're holding on for dear life, you know, because you think you're gonna fall out. Well, I was in so much pain that **I would hold on with one hand to the chair—white knuckles—and in the other hand I'm writing this book**. And I'd sit there for the first—next—ten minutes and finally, I said, "This is ridiculous, this is ridiculous [laughs]." I'd say, "Okay, Lord," you know. And then the devil whispered in my ear and he would tell me, "If you quit working on that book, if you throw away what you've found, I'll leave you alone and you won't be in any pain." And I said, "Get thee behind me, Satan. We're goin' forward with this thing," you know. I said, "In the, ah, Inquisition, people put up with this kind of stuff," and I said, "I can put up with it [laughs], too." ... And, so, **for a period of six years, I worked on the book for about six to eight hours a day**, researching, collating. [21]

First, KSU records show that it is not true that she was on bed rest for the entire nine months of her pregnancy. In the Interior Design records

---

[21] Riplinger lecture: *Testimony, Question & Answer* at a pastor's conference.

section of the KSU Archive Department, there is a letter addressed to the president of the university, Michael Schwartz, from Gail and several of her colleagues. This letter (on file) is dated January 16, 1987 and details the preparation for an impending visit to the KSU Interior Design Department by the Foundation for Interior Design Education and Research (F.I.D.E.R.). This was to be a large event for the KSU Interior Design Department because it was "in the final stages of preparation for the Interior Design accreditation," which they were expecting the F.I.D.E.R to grant to the department.[22] The letter included a "schedule of events" and "the time scheduled" for the president's "meeting with the team."[23] The schedule of events indicates who within the Interior Design Department was responsible for which event while the F.I.D.E.R. was visiting. Along with her colleagues, Gail placed her signature on the letter.[24] The crucial point here is that Gail's signing of the letter to the president clearly indicates that she was at work and not on bed rest for her entire pregnancy, since she was five months pregnant at the date of signing. Contrary to what Riplinger said, not every case of placenta previa requires a woman to be on bed rest for nine months, because the problem often corrects itself before delivery.[25] In fact, the ultrasound equipment of the 1980s was not as

---

[22] Letter addressed to Michael Schwartz, President, dated January 16, 1987, from Theodore F. Irmiter, Ph.D., Acting Director; Daniel H. Giffen, J.D., ASID, Assistant Professor; Mary Kapenekas, IDEC, ASID, Associate Professor; **Gail Ludwig, ASID, Assistant Professor**; and Gretchen Steensen, Instructor. The letter is signed by Gail in her signature (copy on file).
[23] Ibid.
[24] The signature matches Gail's signatures on her various legal documents.
[25] *Placenta Previa* is a complication of pregnancy where the baby's placenta partially or completely blocks the opening of the uterus (cervix), which can interfere with the baby's delivery. A partial blockage has a 90% chance of correcting itself (moving and unblocking) before delivery while a complete blockage does not always correct itself and carries a higher risk for cesarean delivery of the baby. For the complete form, as the baby grows larger, some women are placed on bed rest around 6 months as a precaution, to prevent bleeding and premature birth. Placenta previa occurs more often in pregnant women over the age of 35. Due to the poorer visibility of earlier ultrasound equipment in the 1980s (Riplinger's daughter was born in 1987), the

clear as it is today and the diagnosis of placenta previa could seldom be confirmed until the third trimester of pregnancy (around the sixth or seventh month).[26] If she went on bed rest, it would have been sometime after the date of the letter. The letter and the lesser ultrasound clarity in 1987 both indicate that Gail did not spend her entire pregnancy in bed. In addition, KSU records show that she taught two Interior Design courses during the spring of 1987,[27] not long before her daughter was born. So, why did she lie to the pastor's at the conference by telling them she was bedridden for the entire nine months? Because she figured they knew nothing about placenta previa and would be manipulated emotionally into feeling sorry for her and, therefore, would just believe everything she told them?

The lies do not stop here. It is also untrue that after she had her daughter (1987) she did not go back to work. KSU records show that Gail took the summer of 1987 off,[28] following the birth of her daughter, and then she returned to teach Interior Design during the Fall Semester of 1987, the Spring Semester of 1988, and the Summer Semester of 1988.[29] She left KSU following the Summer Semester of 1988.[30] This also indicates that the "six years" she constantly refers to for her time of disability and research were actually four-and-a-half years, counting from the time she left KSU (Fall of 1988) until March of 1993, when *New Age Bible Versions* was first printed. Why the false story?

"diagnosis of placenta previa [could] seldom be confirmed until the third trimester [at 6 to 7 months of pregnancy]" (from *Essentials of Maternity Nursing, The Nurse and the Childbearing Family*, Second Edition, 1987, The C.V. Mosby Company, p. 731). So, it is highly unlikely that Riplinger would have had to be on bed rest for the entire nine months.

[26] *Essentials of Maternity Nursing, The Nurse and the Childbearing Family*, Second Edition, 1987, The C.V. Mosby Company, p. 731

[27] The Kent State University schedule of classes by semester, obtained from the KSU Archive Department.

[28] Ibid.

[29] Ibid.

[30] Ibid.

Second, if a person is having pain that is "beyond 50 on the Richter scale" due to a disabling disorder, her doctor will most likely show mercy by putting her on good pain-control medication. In addition to making life bearable to some degree, these medications more often than not make a person very drowsy, which means they often end up spending more time asleep than awake. Such a person is going to have limited ability to think clearly, very little time to collate Bibles, and have far less time and ability to care for a "little baby" or young child. If Riplinger could not "see very well," how in the world did she spend "eight to twelve hours a day" looking at Bibles and documents? If her hands did not work well, how was she able to sufficiently hold onto her chair with one weak hand while writing with the other, and hold herself up, all at the same time? Between pain meds and a disabled body, Gail would have been at a tremendous risk of falling, which would have made her bed the safest place for her, not a chair. Even if pain medicine might have made it easier to move, it would still have made it next to impossible to sit up safely in a chair—especially for eight to twelve hours a day—due to the drowsy effects of the medicine. A person who cannot turn herself in bed is not likely capable of sitting up in a chair at all. If she could not walk, how could she get into a chair? She does not mention her husband's or anyone else's assistance. She seems to imply she did all this by herself. Again, how did she care for her young daughter? Riplinger's contradictions only stir up more questions.

Third, to what "God" was she referring? The God of the Bible is a God of perfect order, mercy, and design. When He gives a person a task of great measure, His equipping him or her to do the task is proportionate to the call. In other words, as shown in scripture, He has never cut off a person's legs and arms and then sent them to go defeat an army. He equips them to do the battle, giving to them and not taking from them. When God called David to kill Goliath, He equipped David with fingers that were firmly able to hold and maneuver the slingshot. God is neither the author of confusion nor a liar.

Riplinger's account of "God" talking to her appears comedic and unrealistic, and mocking of God's intelligence and character. God does not slam someone with a terrible disability and then banter comically with that person, demanding they get up do something which He has made it next to impossible for them to do. He is a God of mercy toward those that are His children. The God of the Bible is not some cruel, apathetic joker, which is what the "God" in Riplinger's story appears to be. His trials fit His cause and His punishments always fit the crime. The God of the Bible is exactly as He appears in the Scripture; He does not change. By the time Riplinger got to the part about working on the book late at night, she only identified "God" as "he." She said "he" told her to "get up and work on the book." Who is "he"? With both "God" and "the devil" talking to her, how was she able to keep the voices straight? Was it the pain medicine making her believe she heard "God" talking? Given that she has blatantly lied about God's word and other people in *New Age Bible Versions* (which will be proved in this book), Christians can be confidence that it was not the voice of the God of the Bible commanding her to "get up and work on the book." With the many errors in it, God certainly did not tell her that it was going to be "his book," since God is eternally perfect and cannot make errors. To Christians this should be logical.

Examining the Variations in Her Disability Story

As already seen in some versions of Riplinger's story, she said she *never* left her house, except for doctor visits to the Cleveland Clinic, and that she "could not go to the library." Did she take her bed with her on those research trips to the New Age bookstore and KSU library? One has to wonder how Riplinger acquired much of her materials if she was confined to her bed, immobile, could not see, and was in such extreme pain. For example, in footnote 23 of chapter 42 in *New Age Bible Versions*, she cites the "Munich edition" of a German source. The supposed six-year period of her research was before the convenience of the Internet. Between 1987 and 1993 the Internet, at least as we know it today, was practically non-existent. How did she learn of or obtain such a resource when there was yet no World Wide Web and she was unable to "go to the library"? During this time, Kent State University probably had an early, basic version of intranet connecting it to other universities. However, in order to find the books and other materials she used in the writing of *New Age Bible Versions*, she would have had to go to KSU to access such a connection. Searching for resources would have taken many hours per day. Reality and the contradictions cast doubt upon the "disability" story—or at least the severity of it. Did she think that some people would not catch the contradiction or ask questions?

Unfortunately, the contradictions do not end here. In several other interviews, Riplinger forgot about her "disability" altogether when talking about her six years of research and collation:

In the *Nite Line* (*New Age Bible Versions*) Interview, 1995:

> I prayed to the Lord and I said, "Lord, I need some time to look at these versions." I said, "This needs to be a word-for-word collation"—I like to be thorough in things I do—"We need to start, you know, first word of the first sentence of the new versions and go right through. I want to see what's happening, why have these changes taken place." And, so, the Lord was so gracious, um, and I **spent the next <u>six years</u>, between, ah, four and <u>twelve hours a day</u>**—more often **<u>twelve hours</u> than four hours—for six years**, collating word-for-word the new versions of the Bible, comparing them with the Authorized King James Version. ... And, so, that's how the *New Age Bible Version* book came to be. ... I would stay up late at night—and by two or three o'clock in the morning—and **I'd wanna <u>go run</u> and wake up my husband** and say, you know, "Look what they've taken out." I was just so upset. ... It took me a year-and-a-half just to do the New American Standard Bible—**<u>twelve hours a day</u>**, comparing it with the King James. Then I went on to

do the underlying Greek texts. I found out about the differences in the Greek text and then I started looking back at the manuscripts. And **altogether it took six years**.[31]

In the KNIS Radio interview, in the mid 1990s (sold on CD by Riplinger):

> The book *New Age Bible Versions* sprung out of loving concern for some students of mine from Kent State University. It seemed that those who used the new versions, like the NASB or NIV, were beset by emotional problems or difficulties in their walk with the Lord and, ah, a quick and comforting cure came as they switched to the Authorized King James Version. **This mysterious phenomena [sic], repeated year after year, catapulted me into an exhaustive six-year collation of new Bible versions ...I sat down for twelve hours a day**, comparing the King James Version to the New American Standard Version.[32]

This time it was not "God" who "catapulted" her into the six-year collation via pregnancy or a disability but a "mysterious phenomenon" having to do with her students. In fact, "God" and any prayers said were completely left out of this explanation. She said she "sat down for twelve hours a day." One has to be able to stand in order to "sit down," which is an act of volition. She mentioned nothing about an inability to walk, see, or use her hands, or the white-knuckled attempts to hold herself up in a chair. This time, she also left out any mention of having just had a risky pregnancy condition and a new baby. Her story seems to change, depending on her audience. Did she leave out her "disability" story in these two accounts because she was actually *never*

---

[31] *Nite Line features New Age Bible Versions* (video), an interview with Gail Riplinger, c. 1995, Dove Broadcasting, Inc., P.O. Box 1616, Greenville, SC 29602. Sold by Gail Riplinger and Chick.com.
[32] This interview is sold by Riplinger's A.V. Publications, Corp.

severely debilitated at all and she thought no one would notice the different story?

On November 19, 2009, Riplinger gave a radio interview in which she was, again, asked about how she came to write *New Age Bible Versions*. Here is her answer:

> Well, I know *New Age Bible Versions* **took about six years to write**, about **eight hours a day**. I would start working at about 10 o'clock at night and work 'til three o'clock in the morning. **I didn't want it to be an interruption to my caring for my daughter**—who was a young child at the time—**or my caring for my family** and, so, **I did it late at night**, which I think [laughs] I—**I went to the doctors after a number of years**—I was very ill—and he said, 'Well, you have all the symptoms of [laughs] sleep deprivation [unintelligible], so that was interesting.[33]

Nearly 14 years after the church lectures, her story changed from collating and researching for mostly "twelve hours a day" to "eight hours a day." Her diagnosis of a severely debilitating, painful "connective tissue disease," which required her to retire from her job, changed to "sleep deprivation." She completely left out any mention of a "six-year" "disability" or being "bed-fast." In this version of the story, she did not go to the doctor until *after* "a number of years" rather than *during* the six years ("Cleveland Clinic"), as she had told the congregation of Gospel Light Baptist Church in the 1990s. And, this time, she mentioned "caring" for her "daughter" and her "family" while she did her research. How did she "care" for her daughter? Where did the inability to turn herself in bed, the difficulty seeing, the terrible pain, and the inability to get out of bed go? After all these years, did she forget to tell the "disability" story? Or was she hoping

---

[33] Radio interview on the morning program *The Rise & Shine Time*, WBLW radio, 88.1 FM, Grace Baptist Church, Gaylord, MI, November 19, 2009 (on file).

that everyone else has forgotten about it? *Things that are different are not the same.* So, which story is true?

Let us compare the numerous contradictions seen in her varying stories:

Riplinger's Various Statements	The Contradictions
"I developed a connective tissue disease," "I have a connective tissue disease and that's what allowed me to do a **six-year collation of new Bible** versions"	Although she says she had a connective tissue disease that caused disability and unbearable pain, she somehow managed to collate multiple Bibles for 8 to 12 hours a day, for six years?
"I couldn't walk"	"[A]t night I could go out a little bit," "I'd get up and work on [the book]," "I didn't want [the collating] to be an interruption to my caring for my daughter—who was a young child at the time—or my caring for my family…"
"I couldn't see very well"	She somehow read small print and collated multiple Bibles for 8 to 12 hours a day? "I used to look out the window at the little old ladies…" "I didn't want [the collating] to be an interruption to my caring for

Riplinger's Various Statements	The Contradictions
Cont'd	my daughter—who was a young child at the time—or caring for my family…"
"I could hardly use my hands," "I couldn't grasp a pencil with my hands," "I couldn't use my thumbs"	Despite hands and thumbs that did not work well or were unusable, and being unable to grasp a pencil (pen), she managed to write down notes and the manuscript for her book?

WHO IS GAIL RIPLINGER? | 91

	She said she would "hold on with one hand to the chair…and in the other hand I'm writing this book," "I didn't want [the collating] to be an interruption to my caring for my daughter—who was a young child at the time—or caring for my family…"
"In…absolute pain…beyond 50 on the Richter Scale," "I was in so much pain"	"I worked on the book for about six to eight hours a day," "I'd get up and I'd work on [the book]," "[A]t night I could go out a little bit," "I didn't want [the collating] to be an interruption to my caring for my daughter—who was a young child at the time—or caring for my family…"
"I couldn't go to the library"	"On one of my infrequent research visits to the local New Age bookstore…," "On today's visit to the Kent State University bookstore…," "Much digging in libraries and manuscripts from around the world," "[A]t night I could go out a little bit."
"I was bedridden for six years," ""I was completely bed-fast for six years"	"[A]t night I could go out a little bit," "I'd get up and I'd work on [the book]," "I would sit there in that chair, for six years," "On one of my infrequent research visits to the local New Age bookstore…," "On today's visit to the Kent State University bookstore…," "Much digging in libraries and manuscripts from around the world…," "I didn't want [the collating] to be an interruption to my caring for my daughter—who was a young child at the time—or

92 | WHO IS GAIL RIPLINGER?

Riplinger's Various Statements	The Contradictions
	caring for my family…"
"[I] never left the house for six years, other than to go to the doctors…"	"On one of my infrequent research visits to the local New Age bookstore…," "On today's visit to the Kent State University bookstore…," "Much digging in libraries and manuscripts from around the world…," "[A]t night I could go out a little bit,"
"I couldn't move," "I couldn't turn over in bed"	"at night I could go out a little bit," "I'd get up and I'd work on [the book]," "I would sit there in that chair, for six years," "On one of my infrequent research visits to the local New Age bookstore…," "On today's visit to the Kent State University bookstore…, ""I didn't want [the collating] to be an interruption to my caring for my daughter—who was a young child at the time—or caring for my family…"
"I had to keep my head under a pillow"	"I used to look out the window at the little old ladies…," "I'd get up and I'd work on [the book]," "[I]n the course of laying in bed for six years, [I] collated word-for-word every single word in the new versions," "I didn't want [the collating] to be an interruption to my caring for my daughter—who was

Riplinger's Various Statements	The Contradictions
Cont'd	a young child at the time—or my caring for my family…"
"I couldn't go out to the mailbox"	"at night I could go out a little bit," "on one of my infrequent research visits to the local New Age

	bookstore...," "on today's visit to the Kent State University bookstore..."
"Other than going to the doctor a few times, for about six years I was in the house"	"On one of my infrequent research visits to the local New Age bookstore...," "on today's visit to the Kent State University bookstore..."

Kent State University was farther from Gail's house than her mailbox, yet while she said she couldn't even go to the mailbox, she somehow managed to go to the KSU library, etc. She was completely disabled and could not even move herself in bed, yet somehow she was able to care for her daughter and family. Based on her stories, Gail Riplinger is an unreliable historian. When the different variations of her "six-years" story are compared, what appears is a fantastical tale of unrealistic events and proportion. She would truly have had to be superhuman to do all of what she claims she did during her research period. The details of her "disability" story resemble those of a person with a *martyr complex*. It is time that her defenders stop making excuses for her and call on her to speak the truth with her neighbors.

Similar contradictions occur in the tribute written by her daughter in the September 2009 *Landmark Anchor*:

> **She could not walk and had been bedridden** for as long as I had known her...When she quit [Kent Sate University] to be **a full-time mom** to me...I was to be the recipient of all that love... [34] [Emphasis added]

Again, it has to be asked: How on earth did Gail Riplinger care for a young child, care for her family, collate the "new versions" for "twelve ("eight") hours a day", all while being bedridden, unable to walk, unable to see well, unable to use her hands, unable to go to the library,

---

[34] The *Landmark Anchor*, September 2009, edited by Mickey Carter of the Landmark Baptist Church, Haines City, FL.

and while in extreme pain that was "50 on the Richter scale"? Simply put, a woman who is bedridden and incapacitated, who cannot move herself in bed—who cannot even care for herself—is not able to be a "full-time mom" in the sense meant by her daughter. Over the past decade, she has told two vastly opposing stories: one of being bedridden for six years and one of obviously not being bedridden. Either she had as severe a disability as she has claimed in some places, and was unable to care for her daughter and family, or she was able to care for her daughter and family because she did not have a severe disability. Both accounts cannot be true. Which one is? Did she make up the "disability" story to *emotionalize* her supporters toward feeling sorry for her? To gain their trust so that they would believe what she has written in her books? To increase book sales? Since her daughter was too young to remember what happened when she was a baby, did her mother lie to her about what actually happened?

It is not impossible or unlikely that Gail had, or has, some kind of health problem, but she has exaggerated it to her audiences, for her own benefit.

The God of the Bible (to whom she credits the writing of *New Age Bible Versions*) is not the author of confusion. Which of Riplinger's accounts is true and why did she make up the other? The story changes, depending on the time, the place, and to whom she is talking. The contradictions are an elephant in the room. Either she did not have this "disability" or, if she did have some sort of "connective tissue disease," it was not nearly as severe or debilitating as she has at times claimed. Either way, why has she not been honest to those who put their trust in her?

Trying to Discredit Those Who Expose Her by Denying the Irrefutable Evidence

When Mrs. Waite asked Gail Riplinger if the report of her divorces was true, she told the Waites that those who had reported the divorces were not credible because they had stated that she was "the only child born to her parents." Riplinger then claimed she had "two sisters."[35] However, this was a ploy to keep her followers on the path with her. If she could make those who had exposed her secret look like they had no clue of what they were talking about, she could make the facts look like a lie while she would continue to appear credible to her defenders. But again, we turned to Riplinger's words from the past to prove that, yet again, she was lying about herself to cover up the fact that her divorces were real. In the *Nite Line* video interview, Riplinger was asked to tell a little bit about herself. This is a portion of what she said:

> I'm an only child and I was raised in Ohio... [36]

Did she think her own words would not come back one day to testify against her? Does she care? In the place of repentance, she chose to quash the truth and further the covering of her divorces with yet more lies. A second witness that testifies to her being the only child of her parents is her parents' divorce record, which states that Gail Anne Ludwig was the only child born during said marriage.[37] Her mother never remarried. If Riplinger indeed has "two sisters," they are half sisters. Her father was married once before he married her mother. If he had any children with his first wife, they would be half-siblings. The subject at hand was that Riplinger was the only child born to her

---

[35] Dr. D.A. Waite reported this live via the Internet, during a question and answer session, at his Bible conference in Princeton, NJ, January 2008.

[36] *Nite Line presents New Age Bible Versions* (video), an interview with Gail Riplinger, c. 1995, Dove Broadcasting, Inc., P.O. Box 1616, Greenville, SC 29602. This video can be purchased through Riplinger's A.V. Publications, Corp.

[37] Divorce document No. 51471, Helen Ludwig vs. Wilson Ludwig, Franklin County, Ohio. Gail was five months old when her mother filed for divorce from her father. The divorce was granted on May 12, 1948, when Gail was seven months old. Although it has been claimed by Gail's daughter that Gail's father would get drunk and beat the infant Gail, when Gail's mother filed for divorce from her father, she did not state "habitual drunkenness" or "extreme cruelty" but "gross neglect of duty," which usually means failure to support the family. After the divorce, her parents became estranged, with her father dying alone in Louisiana, in 1949.

parents, not whether she has any half-siblings. What she was trying to do was fabricate a rabbit trail away from the facts, to make those who were telling the truth about her seem as if they did not know what they were talking about, when in fact they did know. Whether those who reported her divorces were correct or not about her being the only child of her parents in no way negates the reality of her unscriptural divorces.

Why do some still choose to put their trust in a person who has no qualms about lying whenever it suits her? She has refused, repeatedly, to repent, choosing to lie about the truth rather than acknowledge it and obey God. Pastors, where does scripture say it is permissible to defend God's word through the works of an unrepentant, deceitful woman? Does God excuse lying in certain circumstances? What does the King James Bible say? Can we righteously defend the KJV through unrighteous means?

Gail Riplinger's Academic Credentials

They speak vanity every one with his neighbour:
With flattering lips and with a double heart do they speak.
    –Psalm 12:2

While it is true, as Riplinger has said, that "academic credentials have never been God's criteria for using a person,"[38] it is also true that God does not permit a person to lie about, or exaggerate, his or her credentials, as if to gain favor with others or to appear more impressive than they are. There is a difference between what Riplinger *claims* her academic credentials are and what her academic credentials *actually* are. Of the Bible Answer Man, Riplinger said, "It is apparent the host did not put 'study' into his answer regarding my credentials." While

---

[38] Gail Riplinger with Noah Hutchings, *Which Bible is God's Word?*, Hearthstone Publishing, Ltd., 1994, p. 6.

that may or may not be the case, *we* went straight to an accurate source: Riplinger's former employer, Kent State University, for answers concerning her credentials. We will outline some of her claims and then show the reader what the university records indicate.

Her "Six College Textbooks"

The back covers of Riplinger's books, such as *New Age Bible Versions* and *The Language of the King James Bible*, state:

> About the author: ... As a university professor, the author ... authored **six college textbooks** ...

The "About the Author" section in *In Awe of Thy Word* states:

> As a university professor with graduate faculty status, the author...authored **six college textbooks**... [39]

First, it needs to be pointed out that although Riplinger has often mentioned her "six college textbooks" in lectures and interviews, she has never stated their titles. The most likely reason for this is that they were published under her second married name: Gail Kaleda. If she had made it easy for people to find the textbooks, by giving their titles, people might have wondered about her different last name and then discovered that she was hiding two unscriptural divorces. During our research, we found her six textbooks. Their titles are:

1. *Restaurants: a Guide for Architects, Designers and Developers* (published originally as her M.F.A. thesis, 1983).

2. *Plants & Interiors: Guide for Environmental Designers* (publication year not specified).

---

[39] Gail Riplinger, *In Awe of Thy Word*, A.V. Publications, Corp., 2003, p. 1178.

3. *Design Process: A Guide for Designers & Architects* (published 1983).
4. *Form & Space Function: Beginning in Environmental Design* (published 1983).
5. *Visual Merchandising & Store Design* (published 1983).
6. *Offices: A Guide for Designers* (published 1982).

Riplinger has said:

> **On the <u>national level</u>, other universities have received** with enthusiasm **the six college textbooks** I have written. [40] [Emphasis added]

When one hears the words "college textbooks," one might recall the thick, nearly-600-page hardback tomes written by scholars in their field, which many of us were required to study as college students. Such course books are usually printed by national scholastic companies and are known and used in colleges and universities across the United States. Whenever Riplinger mentions her six textbooks, that is often the given impression; yet it is a misleading one. Her textbooks were privately published in soft cover and only a limited number were printed. One cloth-board-binding reference copy of each is archived in the Kent State University library and each title is listed in the Kent State University library card catalog, as well as in the WorldCat.org catalog.[41] None of them are longer than 213 pages. Although she

---

[40] Gail Riplinger with Noah Hutchings, *Which Bible is God's Word?*, op. cit., p. 5.
[41] The Kent State University library lists Gail's textbooks at: http://kentlink.kent.edu/search/X?SEARCH=gail+kaleda &searchscope=1&SORT=D and
http://www.worldcat.org/search?qt=worldcat_org_all&q=gail+kaleda. The WorldCat.org is one of the largest and most complete online catalogs and lists those national libraries that hold copies of whatever books for which one is searching. We own rare copies of *Restaurants* and *Offices*, purchased from a

claims "other universities have received" them "with enthusiasm," no national universities other than the University of Akron[42] hold copies of them. And the only copy held by the University of Akron is *Restaurants: a Guide for Architects, Designers and Developers*.[43] The textbooks were specifically printed for the classes Gail taught and to showcase the research required by Kent State in order to maintain her position on the faculty.[44] Today, these textbooks are hard to find

---

used bookstore in Ohio, and have read *Design Process* and *Visual Merchandising*, at Kent State University.

[42] WorldCat.org: http://www.worldcat.org/title/restaurants-a-guide-for-architects-designers-and-developers/oclc/11165315&referer=brief_results. The WorldCat.org directory lists those national libraries that hold copies of whatever books for which one is searching. Akron University is approximately ten miles from the Kent State University campus.

[43] Ibid.

[44] The Kent State University Promotion Policy at the time that Gail was an instructor states: "Promotion shall be viewed as a recognition of a faculty member's having contributed sustained and distinguished service to the department and/or regional campus to which the faculty belongs. ... Recommendations for promotion shall be based upon to major classes of criteria. The first, and more mechanical one, "Academic Credentials and University Experience," describes the normal minimums of credentials and time-in-rank necessary for promotion consideration. The second, ad by far more important, "Academic Performance and Service," refers to the record of actual performance and the accomplishments by the faculty member in academic and service areas. ... The quality of scholarship and research is important to promotion and is a crucial factor in departments with graduate programs. Research, publication, significant creative activity, the participation and leadership in professional and learned societies and other evidence of outstanding achievement, such as awards, patents, and copyrights, shall be weighed in consideration for promotion. [Such criteria would be] publication of professionally reviewed or refereed articles, monographs, or books in the candidate's field. ... Seeking and securing professionally reviewed research and/or service training grants, especially extramural grants (Policy effective January 24, 1980)." Gail's six textbooks qualified as "monographs in [her] field": the Interior Design aspect of the built environment. Between 1982 and 1983, Gail produced these six works, which according to Kent State records facilitated her promotion, in 1983, from the rank of Instructor to that of Assistant Professor in the Home Economics Department. Gail fulfilled KSU's "research and/or service training grants, especially extramural grants"

outside the Kent State library and have been out of print for over a decade, because they are no longer in use.⁴⁵ The textbooks used in the present Interior Design program at Kent State University are published on the national level by top experts in their field and are actively being sold at such places as Amazon.com and other textbook suppliers. Riplinger's textbooks are not "on the national level."

About one of her textbooks, she has claimed:

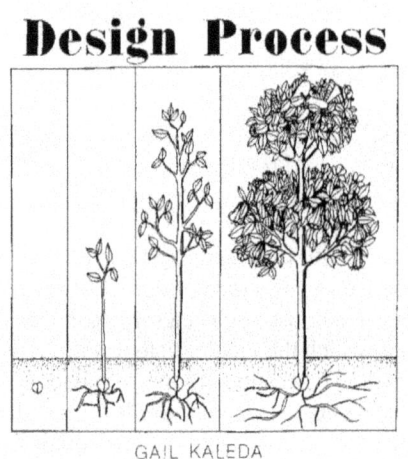
GAIL KALEDA

Now, there's something in one of the textbooks I wrote for—at Kent State University. It was called ***Design Process and Cognitive Behavior***.⁴⁶

One of the textbooks I wrote when I was a professor at the University was **called *Design Process and Cognitive Behavior*.** ⁴⁷

---

promotion requirement when she did her "additional post-graduate study at Harvard and Cornell Universities," as stated on the back cover of *New Age Bible Versions.*

⁴⁵ Kent State University no longer uses Riplinger's textbooks in their Interior Design program and have not for two decades. When we contacted the Kent State University Bookstore, we were told her textbooks have been "out of print for a long time."

⁴⁶ *Research Update, Q & A Session, King James Bible Perfection or NIV, NKJV, NASV Perversion*, lectures recorded at Temple Baptist Church, 2100 W. Woodrow Dr., Knoxville, TN, and televised on the Scripps Howard cable network and WPMC-TV, 1996. This set of lectures is sold by Riplinger's A.V. Publications, Corp.

⁴⁷ *Transparent Translations*, video, recorded at a Prophecy Club conference, filmed at a Kansas City TV station in the mid 1990s and broadcast over television and radio.

> Some years ago a serious investigation into the cognitive processes blossomed into a college textbook on the design process and cognitive behavior (**accepted for publication by Prentice Hall**)... [48] [Parentheses in original]
>
> Some of the textbooks I've written—you had mentioned that I had written six college textbooks—**two of them are about cognitive behavior** and **they were picked up by Prentice Hall**, which is the largest textbook publisher in the United States. [49]

Contradictions once again pop up like glaring red flags, told in Riplinger's own words. In some lectures and interviews, it is *one* college textbook about "cognitive behavior" accepted by Prentice Hall. In another, it is *two* college textbooks that were "picked up by Prentice Hall." Which story is true? The answer is *neither*. Both the textbook title(s) and the "Prentice Hall" claim are *false*. We contacted Prentice Hall to find out. Here is their reply:

> Unfortunately, I don't see any books in our systems by this author. [Email on file]

The assistant at Prentice Hall checked under each of Riplinger's last names used at the time she was at Kent State University and by textbook title.[50] Her textbooks also lack ISBNs.

As can be seen in the list of her six textbooks above, none of them are titled *Design Process & Cognitive Behavior*. That would make seven college textbooks, but there are only "six." She refers to

---

[48] Gail Riplinger, *In Awe of Thy Word*, p. 1178.
[49] *Actions 60s*, with Herman and Sharron Bailey, P.O. Box 6922, Clearwater, Florida, 34618, ©1994. Riplinger's A.V. Publications, Corp. sells this interview series.
[50] The copyright pages of Riplinger's six textbooks do not have Prentice Hall or the name of any other publisher on them. Each textbook was privately printed and copyrighted under the name Gail Kaleda.

New Age Bible Versions as her seventh textbook. The full KSU catalog title is *Design Process: A Guide for Designers & Architects* (the picture above is a scan of this book's title page). As can be seen, the words "cognitive behavior" are nowhere in the title. According to KSU records, Riplinger never taught classes on cognitive behavior or any other course in the field of psychology. I have personally examined each of her textbooks and in not one of them is the central focus on human learning or cognitive behavior—although several feature a *small* section about the psychology of the customer/consumer, which is to be expected. Each of her textbooks are in the field of Interior Design.

The U.S. Copyright Office has no listing for college textbooks by Gail Ludwig, Latessa, Kaleda, or Riplinger. However, when a person says he or she has had college textbooks accepted by "the largest textbook publisher in the United States," it sounds rather impressive, although in reality it is not true. Perhaps Gail did not expect anyone would verify her claims. Does she worry that unless she exaggerates her claims, people might not find her credible?

Her Degrees

The back covers of *New Age Bible Versions, Which Bible is God's Word?, The Language of the King James Bible* and the "About the Author" section of *In Awe of Thy Word*, point out:

> G.A. Riplinger has B.A., M.A., and M.F.A. degrees...

She has never publicly specified what these degrees are in. According to Kent State University, which Riplinger has identified in nearly every interview and lecture as the college at which she studied and then worked as a "professor," her degrees, years obtained, and majors are as follows:

- Bachelor of Arts (1978): Interior Design - Undergraduate [51]

- Master of Arts (1980): Home Economics - Graduate [52]

- Master of Fine Arts (1983): Art - Graduate [53]

These are the only degrees that Kent State University lists for Gail Ludwig Kaleda Riplinger.[54] When the host of *Action 60s* asked her about her degrees, she said:

> My degrees are *not* in Home Economics. [55]

While not *all* of her degrees are in Home Economics, her M.A. *is*. Interestingly, in this interview, Riplinger went into detail about what her degrees are *not* in but failed to answer the question, never telling the host what her degrees are in. Why is that? She did say that anyone could contact her and ask, and that she would be willing to tell them. But why she did not tell the show's host when he was sitting right there asking her, is a bit puzzling. In 2009, when we contacted her

---

[51] *Kent State University Commencement* program, June 10, 1978. The B.A. Interior Design program at KSU is a four-year program. On file in the KSU Archive Department.
[52] *Kent State University Commencement* program, May 24 & 25, 1980. On file at the KSU Archive Department. The M.A. in Home Economics was her first graduate degree and enabled her to be hired as an Instructor at KSU to teach Interior Design, which was part of the Home Economics Department at the time.
[53] *Kent State University Convocation for Graduate Candidates*, August 20, 1983. On file in the KSU Archive Department. This degree was Gail's terminal degree.
[54] These were the last names she used during her time at Kent State University.
[55] *Action 60s* interview, Part Two, op. cit.

home-based company, A.V. Publications,[56] via email, to ask her what her degrees are in, the anonymous person who wrote back curtly stated: "Mrs. Riplinger is not available at this email address. This is AV Publications," then proceeded to ask for our "full name and address," saying, "We will ask her to write to you as time allows." It is puzzling why in the day of lightning fast email, one would need to give his or her address in order to receive a reply to a simple question. As of the printing of this book, we have not yet heard back from Mrs. Riplinger. It is difficult to accept as true that she cannot be reached at an email address that goes to a computer in her own home.[57] Again, we ask, why does she seem reluctant to answer questions about the degrees she so proudly displays on nearly every one of her books?

In the same interview, she stated:

> My terminal degree **is in Industrial and Environmental Design**...[58]

This is untrue. First, let us define what a "terminal degree" is:

> T]he highest degree in a given field of study...in the United States...[59] In order to be called a terminal degree, it must be the highest level of instruction offered in a given field.[60]

---

[56] Commonwealth of Virginia corporate registration records show that Gail Riplinger and her husband own A.V. Publications, Corp., and it is registered and run from the Riplinger house address in Ararat, VA.

[57] The name of the computer from which A.V. Publications' emails originate is "Riplinger1."

[58] *Action 60s*, Part Two, op. cit. During the *Testimony* interview she gave with Mrs. Waite, 1995, Riplinger stated the untruth: "My terminal degree in the area that I taught in, a terminal degree was an M.F.A., or a Masters of Architecture, and, so, I have an M.F.A. in Industrial and Environmental Design." The terminal degree for Interior Design, which was her major, is not in Architecture—not at Kent State University. For some reason, Riplinger passes herself off as more than she actually is.

[59] Wikipedia.com, "Terminal Degree."

[60] EHow.com, "What Is a Terminal Degree in Education?" http://www.ehow.com/about_5260706_terminal-degree-education.html]

In the KNIS Radio interview, she said:

> [I] finally ended up with **a major in Industrial Design**.

And in the interview, *Testimony*, which she gave with Mrs. Waite in 1995, she said:

> My terminal degree—in the area that I taught in, a terminal degree was an M.F.A., or a Masters of Architecture, and, so, **I have an M.F.A. in Industrial and Environmental Design**. And for those who don't know, Industrial Design is, ah, designing products: cars, boats, watches—anything that's a product, that's what an industrial designer does. And I specialized in the area of the environment...large-scale space planning."

Why could she not just honestly state her degrees when asked? She, again, avoided stating the "area" in which she taught. Why? She interrupted herself before she could say what her terminal degree is in and then shifted instead to the terminal degree in the area in which she "taught." What she did not say is that the area in which she taught is the same area in which she has her major: Interior Design, as shown at the beginning of this section. She never mentioned "Interior Design." During the time that she taught at Kent State University, the Interior Design Program was housed primarily in the Home Economics Department, as KSU course books from the early to mid 1980s indicate. In the 1970s and 80s, Home Economics was an allied discipline of Interior Design, and vice versa. Here is how the KSU course book from 1982 describes the program:

> **Interior Design:** The needs of humanity which can be fulfilled by the design of one's surroundings are stressed in a program which **trains interior designers** to identify, research, and creatively solve problems relative to the function and quality of one's near environment. ... Students will be required to maintain a minimum 2.5 accumulative grade-point average in

> the major which includes courses in the Schools of Home
> Economics, Art, Architecture, and Technology. (pp. 187-88).

In 1983, the KSU Home Economics Department was renamed the Department of Family and Consumer Studies, now split into the Lifespan Development & Educational Sciences and Family and Consumer Sciences Education, which is no longer connected with the Interior Design program. The Interior Design program is now housed solely within the KSU School of Architecture and Environmental Design. These programs and schools have changed and advanced over the last two decades, with Family and Consumer Studies branching off into the focus areas of Counseling and Human Development, Educational Psychology, Gerontology, Rehabilitation Counseling, Food Management Production and Services, and other human services. The KSU Interior Design program no longer includes Home Economics type courses in its course of study. For example, classes on Textiles, which used to be Home Economics courses for Interior Design students, are now ID 24510 Textiles in the Built Environment and ID 44512 Historic Furnishing Textiles. The Theory of Architecture is now the Survey of Architectural History.

After Gail majored in Interior Design (B.A, 1978), she went back to KSU to specialize in Home Economics (M.A., 1980), which facilitated her hiring as an Interior Design instructor. After Gail obtained her M.F.A. in Art (1983, terminal degree), it enabled her to teach some of the Art courses required within the Interior Design program, such as Art History I and II.[61]

Contrary to her repeated claim, she has no major in "Industrial and Environmental Design" (KSU has never had a combined major called "Industrial and Environmental Design") and her terminal degree is not a Master of Architecture. The terminal degree for Interior Design

---

[61] KSU Bulletin (course book) for 1982-83, p. 188. She was teaching one of these art classes when she met Michael Riplinger's sister, who was majoring in Crafts at the time.

is indeed the M.F.A.,[62] but it is not the Master of Architecture.[63] As KSU records indicate, the Master of Architecture is the terminal degree only of the Architectural major. As will be explained further in this chapter, although they often work together, Interior Design and Architecture are separate majors and fields.

Industrial Design and Environmental Design (Interior Design and Architecture) are separate degrees. Interior Design deals with the interior of the built environment while, as Riplinger correctly stated, Industrial design deals with the design of products, such as appliances, boats, automobiles, etc. While she would have been required to take a few classes in the area of Industrial Design (such as TECH 11071 Woods Technology I and TECH 11084 Industrial Arts Design I), KSU records show that she certainly did not major in it. In other words, Riplinger has no degrees (minors or majors) specifically in "Industrial Design."[64] She was never hired into the Architecture Department but into the Home Economics Department, and only after obtaining her first graduate degree (1980).

During the same interview with Mrs. Waite, Riplinger misrepresented classes she taught at KSU:

> I ended up teaching at Kent State in—I taught three years for the School of Architecture. I taught the Theory of Architecture I, Theory of Architecture II, Theory of Architecture III. I also taught a course called—for the School of Architecture and Environmental Design called Interior Architecture.

She cut herself off just before she was about to state in which department she taught when she "ended up teaching at Kent State."

---

[62] The terminal degree in Interior Design is the M.F.A.
[63] According to Kent State University alumni records, her M.F.A. is in Art, and at Kent State University, the terminal degree for Interior Design is a M.F.A.
[64] Ibid. A very limited number of Technology classes were required of Interior Design students at KSU in the 1970s and 80s, when Gail was there. It is the same today in the KSU Interior Design program.

She shifted immediately to saying she taught for the School of Architecture. This is false. Kent State records show she did not teach Architecture courses—especially not the Theory of Architecture I, II, and III. Those courses were taught within the Architecture Department and by the Architecture professors listed in the KSU Course bulletins during the time Riplinger was employed at KSU. However, for a very limited time, she taught a course in fashion design (as the subject matter of one of her textbooks indicates), which was also a subcategory of the KSU Home Economics Department. Between 1980 and 1988, Gail taught: Interior Design Professional Practice, Studio Problems in Interior Design I, III, and IV, Methods & Materials in Interior Design, Workshop-Store Design (a School of Fashion Design course), Layout & Design-Plant Operation, Home Furnishings (a Home Economics course), and Interior Design Practicum.

Bearing in mind what her degrees *are* in, let us consider these contradictory claims she has made in various lectures and interviews:

Riplinger's Claim	The Facts
1.) "I'm not a registered architect, yet I taught architect-ture for three years." *Action 60s* interview, Part Two	She is not a "registered architect" because she has no degrees in Architecture. Kent State University, as with any professional teaching institution, does not utilize unqualified persons to teach Architecture. They hire trained, licensed architects to teach Architecture. A Master of Architecture (M. Arch) degree is required for one to teach Architecture at the collegiate level.[65] The degrees obtained by successful Architecture students are the Master of Architecture, Bachelor of Science in Architecture, and the Bachelor

---

[65] "Architectural Majors": http://educhoices.org/articles/Architectural_Majors_Career_Options_for_Architecture_Majors.html

WHO IS GAIL RIPLINGER? | 109

	of Architecture. Riplinger holds none of these. As has already been shown, KSU records show she taught Interior Design, Home Economics, and Fashion Design courses. **Interior Design majors do not teach Architecture courses at KSU.**[66] Riplinger's claim is a grandiose exaggeration.
2.) "I taught for the [KSU] School of Architecture and Environmental Design..." *Action 60s* interview, Part Two	This statement is far more accurate than the previous. While both Architecture and Interior Design are both housed in the KSU *School of Architecture and Environmental Design*, interior designers are not qualified to teach Architecture. KSU records show she taught Interior Design courses.
3.) "Now, when I was a professor at Kent State University, for several years I taught architect-ture." The Prophecy Club lecture	See The Facts in example 1 of this chart. Riplinger's story tends to change depending on the place and audience.
4.) "For the first ten years of my academic	Riplinger has frequently claimed in her lectures that she was a professor for 10

---

[66] KSU course schedules do not list Riplinger as teaching Architecture courses. KSU course books show the Architecture Department fully staffed with Architecture professors for the entire eight years that Riplinger taught there.

career I researched and taught in the area of the built environment." *Which Bible is God's Word?*, p. 6 [Emphasis added]	years. Her words, "For <u>the first ten years</u> of my academic career," make it sound as if her teaching career was longer than 10 years. KSU records show she was hired as an "Instructor" in 1980, coinciding with her first Master Degree (M.A. in Home Economics), and left employment by 1988. This shows her teaching career was 8 years, not 10.
5.) "'Steps ordered by the Lord' in a number of directions (from <u>teaching</u> ABCs to <u>architecture</u>), found their destination in this, the ninth textbook." *In Awe of Thy Word*, p. 1178 [Emphasis added]	See The Facts in example 1 of this chart. When the factual evidence is weighed and the truth is seen, what do Christians believe God thinks about someone who lies about *false* "steps ordered by the Lord"? As the facts show, these "steps" were never "ordered by the Lord" because they did not happen the way Riplinger says they did.

Interior Design and Architecture

Interior Design is a branch of Architecture and Environmental Design, yet it is not Architecture, per se. At KSU, Interior Design majors are required to take some basic Architecture courses (such as Architectural History, Architectural Theory, Environmental Technology I, Graphic Design, and Mechanical/Technical Drawing) so that they will be able to communicate and work with architects in the field. (When Riplinger was teaching at KSU, in the 1980s, KSU required Interior Design students studying within the Home Economics aspect to take the Theory of Architecture I and II, and Environmental Technology I.)[67] While interior designers employ some of the basic techniques and knowledge of architects, the two fields have distinct differences:

- **Interior Design:** Emphasizes the quality of **interior spaces** through the inquiry and synthesis of design theory and the application of functional and aesthetic requirements of the built environment while stressing the health, safety and welfare of the public.[68] An interior designer is responsible for **the interior design, decoration, and functionality of a client's space**, whether the space is commercial, industrial, or residential. ... Employers look favorably on those who have studied engineering, design, and art.[69] **[They] plan interior spaces of almost every type of building, including offices, airport terminals, theaters, shopping malls, restaurants.**[70] [Emphasis added]

- **Architecture:** The art or practice of designing and constructing buildings [structures]. An architect is a trained (licensed) professional who is central to the development of both the **planning** and the **design components** that form the basis for the construction of a building (e.g., skyscrapers, schools, hospitals, churches, train stations, houses). ... Professionally, an architect's decisions affect public safety, and thus an architect must

---

[67] According to the Kent State University Bulletins (course books) from 1979 to 1989 (the ones we examined), these were the Architecture courses required for Interior Design students.
[68] Kent State University College of Architectural and Environmental Design, "Interior Design Overview":
http://www.kent.edu/catalog/2010/collegesprograms/ae/index.cfm,
http://www.caed.kent.edu/Academic/id/overview.html.
[69] The Princeton Review, "Interior Designer,"
http://www.princetonreview.com/Careers.aspx?page=1&cid=82]
[70] United States Department of Labor, Bureau of Labor Statistics, "Interior Designers," http://www.bls.gov/oco/ocos293.htm.]

> undergo specialized training consisting of advanced education and a practicum (or internship) for practical experience to earn a license to practice architecture.[71] [Emphasis added]

While an architect is trained in the *planning and designing of buildings* (the built environment) and their structure, an interior designer is trained in designing and improving the *interior environment* of buildings. The principal subject matter of five of Riplinger's six textbooks is that of Interior Design and reflects the Environmental Design courses she was required to take in order to obtain her B.A. in Interior Design. Several of her textbooks can assist the Architecture student where he or she needs to learn about the role of the interior designer and the interdisciplinary relationship of working together on building projects. But Riplinger's textbooks are not architectural textbooks. By exaggerating her claim to say she taught Architecture, did she believe that would make her appear that much more impressive? Whatever her reason, lying about one's credentials is surely not impressive and does not gain favor with God.

In the KNIS Radio interview, she again misstated her major:

> When I went to college, I changed majors a number of different times in, um—finally ended up with **a major in Industrial Design**.

Riplinger's repeated claim of having a major in Industrial Design is *false*. Did she make it up so that anyone attempting verify her real credentials at Kent State University would not know in what correct department to look?

On p. 1178 of *In Awe of Thy Word*, it says:

---

[71] Oxford American Dictionary; WiseGeek.com "What Does an Architect Do?", Wikipedia.org, "Architect," http://en.wikipedia.org/wiki/Architect, and "What Does an Architect Do?" at http://www.his.com/~pshapiro/architects.html.]

> Coursework and experience in how learning takes place began formally some forty years ago while taking college courses in the field of education...

This statement contains a glaring inaccuracy, one that apparently Riplinger did not consider before she published the book. *In Awe of Thy Word* is copyrighted 2003. Backtrack "forty years" from 2003 and you end up in 1963. As mentioned before, Gail Riplinger was born in October 1947. That means she was 15 going on 16 "forty years" before the printing of *In Awe of Thy Word*. Does she expect people to believe that she was "taking college courses in the field of education" at the age of 15, while still in early high school?

Most of Riplinger's books state:

> Gail Riplinger ... **has done additional postgraduate study at Harvard and Cornell Universities**.

Why she continues to advertise this is uncertain, since, along with her degrees, it has nothing to do with the writing of her books on the "new versions" and she has mocked others who have obtained higher education. Now that we know what her graduate degrees are in, this "postgraduate study" is no longer a mystery. Her first graduate degree is in Home Economics, and Cornell University has one of the largest pioneer Home Economics departments in the United States. What better place is there for a Home Economics instructor to go for continuing education and to fulfill Kent State University's academic research requirements? Any academic research at Harvard University would have been for the same reason as at Cornell. Just utilizing the libraries of these institutions could constitute postgraduate study.

It's *Dr.* Riplinger, to You

In her book *In Awe of Thy Word* (p. 1178), Riplinger states:

> [F]or [New Age Bible Versions] the author was honored with a Doctorate from the world's largest church of its kind.

She is referring to Hyles-Anderson College, run by First Baptist Church of Hammond, Indiana, a church formerly pastored by the late Jack Hyles. There is a problem with Riplinger's claim, however. Hyles-Anderson College, which is not accredited, does not maintain a doctoral program and the "Doctorate" to which she refers is an *honorary*. This means the school is not equipped to give doctorates and that any honorary doctorate from them is of no real value. The value and seriousness of a Hyles-Anderson honorary doctorate can be measured by the fact that the school once awarded such to the late John R. Rice's horse.

Despite the lack of doctoral authority at Hyles-Anderson, Riplinger uses the title "Dr." frequently in written form and is referred to as such by pastors who endorse her. In writing the foreword to the second edition of James Sightler's *A Testimony Founded Forever*, she signed her name: "Dr. G.A. Riplinger, B.A., M.A., M.F.A., Honorary Doctor of Humanities…"

Riplinger should really only expect those who hail allegiance to Hyles-Anderson and its non-doctoral program to call her "Dr." Riplinger. Otherwise, the title is useless.

Riplinger's Time at Kent State University

How Long Did She Actually Teach at KSU?

In various places, Riplinger has stated:

> **I was a professor at Kent State University for <u>ten years</u>** … I was a professor there for <u>ten years</u> … And, so, over **a period of <u>ten years</u>** … [72]

---

[72] Berean Baptist Church lecture, first visit, op. cit.

> **I was a professor at Kent State University for <u>ten years</u>** ... And I was there **for <u>ten years</u>**, with graduate faculty status ... I noticed over a period—over **<u>ten years</u>**, ah—that **<u>ten years</u>** at the university, that the young ladies that I was dealing with ... [73]

> As a professor, the young ladies would come into my office ... And, so, during the course of **the <u>ten years</u> I was there**, I had the privilege ... [74]

> And, so, the Lord pulled a joke on Kent State University and had me be **a professor**, and, ah, through a series of events, had me hired as a professor, and **I worked there for <u>ten years</u>**. ... So, **I worked there for <u>ten years</u>** ... [75]

> **I was awarded <u>tenure</u> and <u>graduate faculty status</u>** at the large state university where **I was a full-time professor for <u>a decade</u>.** [76]

At KSU, freshmen graduate students hired to the faculty start at the lowest rank. KSU's successive faculty ranks are "Instructor, Assistant Professor, Associate Professor, and Full Professor." KSU records state Gail was hired onto the faculty in 1980, starting at the rank of Instructor,[77] immediately following her M.A. in Home Economics. This degree qualified her to teach.

---

[73] Temple Baptist Church, Knoxville, TN, Saturday Evening service, lecture, 1996, op. cit.
[74] Gospel Light Baptist Church lecture, Walkertown, NC, with Dr. Wally Beebe present, op. cit.
[75] *Riplinger's Testimony with Questions & Answers,* lecture during pastors' conference, op. cit.
[76] Gail Riplinger with Noah Hutchings, *Which Bible is God's Word?*, op. cit., p. 5.
[77] At the time that Gail was at Kent State University, the school's course books showed year of hire in parentheses next to the name of each teacher, listed by department, followed by each teacher's rank, teaching area, highest earned degree at the time, and school where degree was earned, with year earned. After hire, Gail appeared in the course book as: "KALEDA, GAIL L.

As previously discussed, Riplinger stated she left KSU on a disability retirement, which was around the time of her daughter's birth (late spring 1987). However, KSU records indicate she continued teaching Interior Design and several Home Economics classes until the spring of 1988. If she left KSU at the birth of her daughter, then she was employed there for only seven years. If, as the course books show, she was there until mid 1988, then she was employed there for only eight years. KSU records indicate she was no longer employed there after 1988. Either way, she was employed there as a teacher for less than ten years. Her words appear to indicate another exaggeration, since they do not align with the facts.

Promotion, Tenure, and Graduate Faculty Status

At Kent State University, it takes several years to advance from one rank to the next, due to probationary periods and other required criteria.[78] In 1983, after obtaining her terminal degree (M.F.A.) and successfully completing the required three years as an Instructor, Gail was promoted to "Assistant Professor." At the time she was there, KSU's "two major classes of criteria" for promotion in rank were "academic credentials and university experience" (her B.A. and M.A. degrees and her three years as an Instructor) and "academic

---

(1980), *Instructor, Home Economics*, M.A., Kent State University, 1979." Although she was hired in the summer of 1980, her name did not appear until the 1981 course book.

[78] According to KSU's Promotion Policy during the time she was employed there, a faculty member was eligible for advancement to the rank of Assistant Professor after successful completion of three years as an Instructor and possession of at least the Master's degree. To advance from Assistant Professor to Associate Professor, one had to successfully complete four years as an assistant professor. To advance from Associate Professor to Full Professor, one had to successfully complete five years as an Associate Professor and must possess the terminal degree in his/her discipline. Altogether, it took approximately 12 years of successful advancement to go from Instructor to Full Professor at KSU (1980).

performance and service" (scholarly research and her six textbooks).[79] At KSU, the ranks of Associate Professor and Full Professor are considered senior faculty positions. Gail remained at the rank of Assistant Professor until she left employment, not at KSU long enough for her to advance to the rank of "Associate Professor" or "Full Professor."[80]

It is true that Gail was eventually tenured. At the time she was at KSU, the Tenure Policy stated that an employee with "an initial appointment at the rank of instructor or assistant professor shall carry a probationary period of six years," before tenure could be granted.[81] Since Gail was hired in 1980, she was not eligible for tenure until 1986. The granting of tenure also secured the faculty member's reappointment for the next year. On March 10, 1986, KSU President Michael Schwartz wrote a letter to Gail informing her: "effective with your appointment of the 1986-87 academic year, you will hold tenure in the Department of Family and Consumer Studies [formerly Home Economics]."[82] Faculty tenure records show that it took Gail the same amount of time to obtain tenure as her department colleagues.[83]

As for Graduate Faculty status, she became eligible only after obtaining the terminal degree in her field (M.F.A., 1983) and after

---

[79] KSU Promotion Policy, 1980, 1982.
[80] Texe Marrs, who has highly promoted Riplinger since 1994, has her listed as a former "Associate Professor at Kent State University" in his web advertisement for the sale of *New Age Bible Versions*:
http://www.powerofprophecy.com/, search "New Age Bible Versions." (Copy on file) We wonder whether he misunderstood her rank or if she supplied him with the incorrect rank.
[81] KSU Promotion Policy, 1977. An updated policy can be viewed online at http://www.ken.edu/policyreg/policydetails.cfm?customel_datapageid_19765 29+2038514.
[82] Letter from KSU President Michael Schwartz, March 10, 1986, notifying "Gail L. Ludwig-Riplinger" of tenure appointment, is on file in the KSU Archive Department among the correspondence letters of Michael Schwartz.
[83] These records are available for public viewing in the KSU Archive Department.

"substantial publication of scholarly research," which included her six textbooks.[84]

Names She used at Kent State University

According to KSU records, she used these last names while teaching at KSU:

- **1980-1985:** Gail L. Kaleda (the L representing the fact that she had taken back her maiden name, Ludwig, after her first divorce)
- **1986-1988:** Gail K. Ludwig (the K representing her former married name, Kaleda, following her second divorce when she again took back her maiden name) and Gail Ludwig-Riplinger

Her last name never appeared as *Riplinger* in the course catalogs, even after she married Mike Riplinger in 1984. After she married Mike, her last name was listed as Gail K. Ludwig. What did the "young ladies" who came into her office think about her immoral life, divorcing one husband and quickly marrying another just two months later? What kind of Christian example was that? If Gail was "not women's lib," as she has stated several times, why did she need to retain her maiden name?

---

[84] KSU Administrative Policy Regarding Graduate Faculty (since 1977): http://www.kent.edu/policyreg/policydetails.cfm?customel_datapageid_19765 29=2038523.

Inclusion in *Who's Who*

In addition to the fact that she has never stated in which edition(s) of *Who's Who* she is supposedly listed, there are other discrepancies in her *Who's Who* claims:
On the back cover of *New Age Bible Versions*:

> [The author was] one of fifty educators worldwide included in <u>an international edition</u> of *Who's Who*...

On the back cover of *Which Bible is God's Word?*

> As one of 50 educators worldwide to be selected in <u>an international edition</u> of "Who's Who"...

In *Which Bible is God's Word?*

> On an international level, I have been listed in <u>an edition</u> of *Who's Who*...

On the back cover of *The Language of the King James Bible*:

> The author is in <u>several editions</u> of *Who's Who*...

In the "About the Author" section of *In Awe of Thy Word*:

> The author is in <u>several editions</u> of *Who's Who*.

The question here is, is it "**an edition** of *Who's Who*" or "**several editions** of *Who's Who*"? Is it "an **edition** of *Who's Who*" or "an **international edition** of *Who's Who*"? The story varies, like some of her others. The claim on the back of her first book was singular and, then, with her third book, it was plural. We should wonder which claim is true, at least for truth's sake.

I wrote to several *Who's Who* publications, starting with one of the most popular in America, the *Marquis Who's Who*, which has published the biographical data of professionals and celebrities for "over 100 years."[85] They publish an international variety, as well. Their reply:

> We do not have a Gail Kaleda (or Gail Anne Ludwig, Riplinger) in any Marquis Who's Who publication [including their international publication].

I also contacted the *International Who's Who* (in business since 1928, located in North Carolina)[86] and she is not in their records under any of her last names. In addition, I contacted several other *Who's Who* companies, with the same results. Riplinger's claim, "As one of 50 educators worldwide to be selected in an international edition of 'Who's Who,'" does not make much sense, since the *International Who's Who* selects *more* than "50 educators worldwide" and has for the many decades they have been in business. Their "membership consists of more than 80,000 professionals worldwide."[87] Even if one wanted to verify her International Who's Who claim by looking in a local library, they would not be able to find this *Who's Who*, because the company's "directories are strictly proprietary, for our member's use only." [Emphasis added] They "do not allow them to be in any library other than the Library of Congress."[88] A copy can cost as much as $745!

Riplinger's *Who's Who* claim sounds impressive to the unsuspecting. However, it is rather common for college graduates and all sorts of professionals to be invited or sometimes be referred by their

---

[85] *Marquis Who's Who* web site, the "Our History" section: http://www.marquiswhoswho.com/about-us.
[86] International Who's Who website: "International Who's Who of Professional Educators includes teachers, instructors, professors, and other educators from a variety of institutes of learning," http://www.internationalwhoswho.com/faq.asp#7.
[87] Ibid. FAQ #8, http://www.internationalwhoswho.com/faq.asp#8.
[88] Ibid. http://www.internationalwhoswho.com/faq.asp#12.

colleagues to have their name listed in any particular edition of *Who's Who*. A person has to accomplish no amazing feat to be invited. The central intention of such publications is to entice people to purchase their books or join their organization, to see their names listed. That way, a person can say his or her name is listed in a "famous" publication. For this reason, many professionals refrain from mentioning their *Who's Who* entries in their curriculum vitae. While inclusion in a *Who's Who* may appear impressive on the surface, it is usually, more often than not, a ploy to obtain one's money by using vanity's enticement. Someone has written a blog posting titled *'Who's Who' Ripoff* [sic] *preys on your ego*, which explains it quite well:

> I must be really important, because two "Who's Who" publications have chosen me for inclusion in their publications. The e-mails arrived in my mailbox this week. They read, "Recently you were selected as an inductee into Who's Who. In spite of this, we have yet to receive your information in order to build your basic membership profile. In the business and professional world it isn't what you know, it's who you know ... and who knows you." ... Here's the problem. No one really cares if you are listed in "Who's Who." Really, they don't. It basically means nothing and does not credential you to do anything. And most professionals know that you are simply paying to be included. Save your money. Go to school instead and get a real credential.[89]

From another blog:

> As one blogger posted on the A to Z forum, playing along with the Who's Who request "tells a superintendent that you are

---

[89] Wallet Pop blog, *Who's Who' ripoff* [sic] *prays on your ego*, by Barbara Bartlein, http://www.walletpop.com/blog/2009/11/16/whos-who-ripoff-preys-on-your-ego/.

naive, inexperienced, and provincial. ..."[90]

Who's Who companies solicit most professionals at some point, but like the statements above point out, it means next to nothing about who you are or how educated or successful you are. They make money off people who want their names listed in a book. A *Who's Who* directory can be useful to some professionals as a means of networking with other professionals, but little else. So, if Riplinger happens to be listed in any of the many *Who's Who* publications, it is not all that big of a deal.

Can Riplinger *Read* Greek?

The way Gail Riplinger speaks of examining the Greek texts underlying "new versions," many have been led to believe that she is able to *read* Greek. For example, during the KNIS Radio interview, she said she "collated" different Greek manuscripts during her six years of research. However, she has never actually said, "I can read and understand Greek" or "I am not formally trained in New Testament Greek." Now, let us preface this section by saying that no one needs to be able to read Greek in order to read or understand God's word in their own language. And no one is required to know Greek to study the Bible Version Debate. But if someone talks about collating Greek texts and Bible manuscripts, they need to be sure they are truly able to read Greek, can prove they understand Greek, and be honest about it when asked.

KNIS Radio Interview

During the KNIS Radio interview, host Bill Feltner asked Riplinger:

---

[90] Pedablogue Archives, "Who's Who Among American Teachers," by Michael Arnzen, Ph.D, April 2005, http://blogs.setonhill.edu/MikeArnzen/%20009078.

WHO IS GAIL RIPLINGER? | 123

> Much of the foundation of your book rests on problems with the Greek manuscripts used to produce many of these new versions. **Do you have a background in Greek? Do you *read* or *write* Greek?**

Riplinger's answer:

> Um, well, it's very interesting, I've always had an interest in languages, and when I was growing up, ah, you know, most nine-year-olds are taking baton lessons, and my mother had a Latin tutor for me. So, I've always been very interested in languages and when I was 18, I was hired by a community center to teach, um, foreign language and English to, ah, Greek-speaking people, Russian-speaking people, Italians, Japanese—probably I had six or eight people in my class when I was 18 years old, teaching, um—trying to Americanize them, giving them English lessons. So, I've always been interested in languages. And when I went to college, I changed majors a number of different times and, ah, finally ended up with a major in Industrial Design. But that is—was not necessarily my interest in life.

She did *not* answer the question. The host was not asking her about her interest in languages, her Latin lessons, how many times she changed majors in college, or about her supposed teaching English to foreigners. He asked her if she *reads* or *writes* Greek. He meant "background," as in knowledge of the Greek language, as in a proper education/study in Greek language, in order to be skilled at or fluent in the many complexities of Biblical Greek (its semantics, grammar, morphology, syntax, and phonetics). In other words, if she were to pick up one of thousands of Greek manuscripts, could she actually read it unassisted? Yet, according to her extraneous statement, it is obvious the answer is *no*. Why could she not just say so? Having had a Latin tutor has nothing to do with learning an intimate knowledge of New Testament Greek. Teaching English to a few Greek-speaking people does not make a person an expert in New Testament Greek. Bible scholars are trained for years in Greek and its grammar, etc. If one can learn fluent Greek from simply teaching English to foreigners, then most Greek language students are wasting their money by paying exorbitant tuition costs during years of learning.

In her *Testimony* interview with Mrs. Waite, she said:

> I think there are seminary graduates out there who say they know Greek, and I know more Greek than they do.

Then, in the Action 60s interview, after speaking about teaching English to foreign-speaking people for three years, Riplinger said:

> After you do that for three years, I'm afraid you're going to know the language, whether you intend to or not.

This is utter hogwash. No one truly learns the complexities a language without intending to. No one learns how to read and write Greek after three years of teaching English to foreigners. Her statements are rather insolent in regard to those students who spend years in diligent study, learning to *read* and *write* Greek. Since she hints that she "knows" Greek from having taught English, then she must also be a real expert in Japanese, Italian, Serbo-Croatian, etc., since people who spoke those languages were also part of her class. She must be quite the multilingual expert.

While it is always possible to glean *some* words and common phrases when exposed to another language on a casual basis, this does not by any stretch make one an expert. However, the Greek scholars lambasted by Riplinger in her works are/were experts, with years of intense study to show for themselves. One needs proper, formal training in order to properly understand the many technicalities and depth of New Testament Greek—or any form of Greek. At one of my jobs, I worked with some men from Ghana who spoke German as a second language. Over a period of half a year, I learned some common words and phrases, but this taught me nothing about German grammar, variants, or spelling, and did not make me highly conversant in the language. If I had thought myself an expert in the German language, I would have been fooling myself. I learned enough to be able to ask two of my German-speaking patients if they were hungry, hot, cold, tired, or not feeling well. During some extensive study on the 19th-century Great Famine of Ireland, I learned quite a collection of Irish Gaelic words and phrases, but this in no way made me enough of a Gaelic expert to converse in it or to read books written in it. Riplinger says she also taught English to Russian, Italian, and Japanese people. So, are we supposed to believe this means she learned to read and write those languages, as well? We think not. In some of her lectures, she can often be heard mispronouncing Greek words, which we will discuss later in this book.

Dr. H. Wayne House

Dr. H. Wayne House, apologist and professor of Law and Biblical Studies, engaged in a two-hour debate with Riplinger in 1994. He states that he "had to ask her four times before **she hesitatingly admitted that she really could not *read* Greek**."[91] [Emphasis added] There was the answer, even though it had to be drawn hesitatingly out of her. Is it not interesting that she failed to offer this honest information to Bill Feltner when he asked her during the KNIS Radio interview?

Our question to Gail Riplinger, as it should also be from those who defend her, is:

> Since, obviously, you cannot read Greek on your own, and you have had no formal training in it (tutoring English to Greek and Russian students does not count), and since you have pronounced all Greek-English lexicons as corrupt, then what is

---

[91] *A Summary Critique: New Age Bible Versions, G.A. Riplinger*, by H. Wayne House, Statement DB015, archived at the Christian Research Institute, www.equip.org. (Copy on file)

your source for the definitions of the Greek words you cite in your books and lectures?

Many would like the answer to this question. Until she answers, we believe that it remains enormously obvious that she uses some sort of Greek-English translation tool to obtain the definitions of Greek words, since foreign languages—especially ancient ones—do not come to a person from out of the thin air. We would like her to reveal what tool(s) this would be?

As for the Hebrew, Riplinger is no more educated in it than she is in Greek.

Honor Awards

In her interview with Dr. Noah Hutchings of Southwest Radio Church, as recorded in the book *Which Bible is God's Word?*, Riplinger explained:

My colleagues elected me to membership in a national education honorary. [92]

Which one? There are many. She never states the name. For some reason, she is extremely vague with the information. The back covers of most of her books read:

As a university professor, the author...was selected for the Honor Society's teaching award and membership in a national Education Honorary.

---

[92] *Which Bible is God's Word?*, op. cit., p. 5.

Again, to what "national education Honorary" and to what "Honor Society" is she alluding? There are many. Does she mean a particular honor society specifically affiliated with Kent State? Which one? If the answers to these questions are not important then why does she even bring up the "awards"? Apparently, she believes that mentioning these details is important. The term *honor society* is generic for any rank organization that recognizes academic excellence among peers. Numerous societies of this kind exist in the U.S. to recognize various fields and circumstances.[93] Nearly every notable university has at least one. However, there is no such organization just called "the Honor Society," although we did come across a rock band calling itself that. It would be helpful if Riplinger would state the name of the honor society to which she refers.

"Selected" for the award does not mean she was actually awarded, just that she was selected as a candidate among other selected candidates.

Again, to Noah Hutchings:

> [T]he president of the university awarded me a Mortar Board Honor Society teaching award.[94]

It is difficult to say whether this statement is accurate, as we searched through presidential correspondence in the KSU Archive Department[95]

---

[93] Wikipedia article, "Honor Society," http://en.wikipedia.org/wiki/Honor_Society. The "Honor Societies" picture on p. 66 is an illustration from the 1909 yearbook of the University of Washington. Note the pagan mystery imagery depicted in this emblem, the androgynous figure holding a Roman laurel, with the circle overhead with what appears to be the gnarls of tree branches, and lamp stands on either side. One could argue that to be inducted into such academic societies, one must agree with whatever esoteric background (history) in which they are steeped.

[94] *Which Bible is God's Word?*, op. cit., p. 5.

[95] The correspondence of the presidents of KSU are handled by the KSU Archive Department and contain every piece of correspondence (in boxes) sent and received by the majority of KSU presidents over the decades. Their correspondence is considered part of the preservation of the history of KSU.

and did not find any such award with Gail's name(s) on it. We did find KSU recipients of different types of awards but none that confirmed Gail's claims. There is a Mortar Board National College Senior Honor Society (www.mortarboard.org) to which "a select few students on each campus are invited to join…an honor naming them among the most amazing scholar-leaders in the U.S." However, Riplinger's information is vague, and while it is, perhaps, hard to disprove, it is hard to prove, as well.

Ronald Reagan's Citizen Ambassador Program

The back covers of the first, second, and fourth printings of *New Age Bible Versions* state:

> The author was **invited** by **the President's Citizen Ambassador Program** to be a representative to Russia. [Emphasis added]

From the "About the Author" section (p. 1178) of *In Awe of Thy Word*:

> …an invitation by President Reagan's Citizens Ambassador Program to join a team of U.S. doctors and architects to share research abroad.

Riplinger has never specified whether she was just *invited* or if she actually *went* to Russia (abroad). The vague nature of her claim leads to more questions. Perhaps this is why she changed some of the wording on the back cover of *New Age Bible Versions* with later printings:

> The author was **selected** by **President Reagan's Citizen Ambassador Program** to represent the U.S. abroad.[96]
> [Emphasis added]

---

[96] *New Age Bible Versions*, 12th (2003) through 14th (2005) printings.

WHO IS GAIL RIPLINGER? | 129

She changed "invited" to "selected," "to be a representative to Russia" to "to represent the U.S. abroad" (dropping "Russia"), and she changed "the President's" to "Reagan's" preceding "Citizen Ambassador Program."

In *Which Bible is God's Word?*, she said:

> [I] was invited by President Reagan's Citizen Ambassador Program to be a representative to Finland and Russia.[97]

In this account, she added Finland.

This citizen ambassador program is part of People to People Ambassador International. People to People International was created in 1956 by President Dwight D. Eisenhower and "opened the doors of governments and the homes of private citizens to cultural exchange and international understanding in the belief that people play a significant role in keeping world peace. ... The People to People organization is President Eisenhower's lasting legacy, while created in the 20th century extends into the 21st century promoting world peace through the people of the world."[98] Between 1981 and 1989, People to People was chaired by President Reagan[99] just as it has been by almost every president since President Eisenhower. People to People has several programs: Student Ambassadors, Sports Ambassadors, Leadership, and Citizen Ambassadors. Their web site states:

> The purpose of People to People International is to enhance international understanding and friendship through educational, cultural and humanitarian activities involving the exchange of ideas and experiences directly among peoples of

---

[97] Which Bible is God's Word?, op. cit., pp. 5-6.
[98] "Dwight David Eisenhower, Peace Hero of the 20th Century and Beyond," by John Byron Goodman,
http://www.wagingpeace.org/menu/programs/youth-outreach/peace-heroes/eisenhower-dwight.htm.
[99] People to People Ambassador Programs official web site: www.peopletopeople.com.

different countries and diverse cultures. [100]

and:
> People to People Ambassador Programs offer students, educators, athletes, and professionals unique travel opportunities for personal and professional growth and continuing education. ... With nearly 50 years of experience, more than 400,000 alumni, and destinations on seven continents, People to People is the world's most recognized and respected educational travel provider. [101]

The Citizen Ambassador Program states:
> People to people Citizen Ambassador Programs offers professionals unique travel opportunities that foster local and global networking, career development, personal enrichment, and international goodwill. Citizen Ambassadors intersect with other professionals from around the world and engage in cultural activities, seminars, and humanitarian efforts. [102]

Interestingly, a friend who knew Riplinger in the 1980s does not recall her ever going abroad. So, this could explain the words "selected" and "invited" and why she has never stated she actually *went* abroad. Being "invited" does not mean she actually went. Similar to invitations sent out by *Who's Who* publications, many students receive invites from People to People and some professionals are nominated by others to go on People to People trips. Some people end up receiving an invitation letter because their name has been placed on a mailing list at some point and that list was sold to other companies. There have been incidences where people's dead pets and several deceased children

---

[100] People to People International, "History" page, http://www.ptpi.org/about_us/History.aspx.
[101] People to People Ambassador Programs, "Main" and "About Us" pages, http://www.peopletopeople.com/Pages/default.aspx and http://www.peopletopeople.com/AboutUs/Pages/default.aspx.
[102] http://www.peopletopeople.com/OurPrograms/CAP/Pages/default.aspx.

have received invitations, something which has raised serious questions about some of People to People's marketing tactics. One case involving a deceased child got the attention of the Iowa Attorney General.[103] Would-be Citizen Ambassadors are required to pay their own round-trip transportation, an expense that can be a deterrent to some. Many high school students receive letters from the People to People Student Ambassador division that make it sound as if they have been specially nominated for an educational trip overseas but then their parents soon discover it costs nearly $7,000. Students who received invitation letters telling them they were selected for their high academic achievement have discovered that children in their classes who had a poor academic record received the same invitation.[104]

It appears that Riplinger has mentioned the citizen ambassadorship information, along with the rest, as an attempt to impress her readers.

---

[103] In an Iowa Attorney General (Consumer Protection Division) letter to an attorney for People to People International, misleading information by the group and an invitation sent to a deceased child are addressed. Part of the letter, dated June 8, 2006, states: "As you know, our concerns began when the mother of a child who had died in 1993 at seven weeks of age received a letter last September form People to People inviting her son to 'join other outstanding middle school students from the Des Moines and Central Iowa area who are eligible for People to People...' The letter indicated that her son had been 'recommended for the honor by a teacher, former Student Ambassador or national academic listing.' The letter raised concerns that parents were being led to believe that their child had been chosen for an honor based on recommendations or academic performance, criteria that could not possibly have applied to the infant who died years ago at seven weeks of age." http://www.state.ia.us/government/ag/latest_news/releases/june_2006/People_to_People.html. In another incident, "the Parents of Earl Gray," a deceased cat, received two separate invitation letters from the marketing company for People to People, "Deceased Cat Invited to be Student Ambassador," http://www.consumeraffairs.com/news04/2006/12/p2p_earl.html.

[104] "People to People: Ambassadors or Tourists?" by Lisa Wade McCormick, November 20, 2006, http://www.consumeraffairs.com/news04/2006/11/people_to_people_marketing.html.

Riplinger Claims She is a "Linguistics Expert"

Another credential that Gail Riplinger should scratch off her list is her claim that she is a "linguistics expert." In the Action 60s interview, Riplinger stated:

> And, ah, so far as my background in linguistics, I taught English for three years. Ah, and in my classes, it was English for the foreign born...none of which spoke one word of English, and I had to teach them...the English language. So, of course I, **I became a linguistics expert after three years of doing that**.

In an interview she gave on WBLW Radio (88.1 FM, Grace Baptist Church, Gaylord, Michigan), November 19, 2009, she stated:

> [B]asically, I teach, um, history and linguistics.

First, let us define the terms *linguist* and *linguistics*:

> **Linguistics:** A study of human speech in its various aspects (as the units, nature, structure, and modification of language, languages, or a language including esp. such factors as phonetics, phonology, morphology, accent, syntax, semantics, general or philological grammar, and the relation between writing and speech) – called also linguistic science, science of language; compare with philology. (*Webster's Third New International Dictionary*, Unabridged)

> **Linguist:** 1. A person accomplished in languages and especially in living languages. 2. A student of or expert in linguistics. (*Webster's Third New International Dictionary*, Unabridged)

WHO IS GAIL RIPLINGER? | 133

Riplinger's credentials for being a "linguistics expert" are that she "taught English for three years" to "the foreign born" who spoke Greek, Japanese, Spanish, Serbo-Croatian, Yugoslavian, and Italian. She's said, "So, of course, I became a linguistics expert after three years of doing that."[105] How does three years of teaching English to foreigners make one an expert in language(s)? It doesn't. It takes years of proper training to be a good linguist and once this has been accomplished, a person will be able to satisfactorily demonstrate their linguistic expertise. Being around foreign-speaking people for three years is not going to make this happen. Riplinger did not become a "linguistics expert" any more than she learned to read and write Greek during those three years.

The main problem with Gail Riplinger referring to herself as a "linguistics expert" is that she has demonstrated a chronic inability, throughout her lectures and interviews, to correctly pronounce certain words with which one such as herself should be well familiar. The following is an example of some of the words she mispronounces:

The Correct Word with Correct Pronunciation	How Riplinger Mispronounces the Word
Papyri (*pah' pie rye*)	Paprah;[106] Papyrah[107]
Samaritan Pentateuch	In some lectures she has called it the "Sumerian Pentateuch."[108] [A Samaritan and a Sumerian are not the same, as Samaria and Sumer are/were in different geographical locations and time periods. There

---

[105] *Action 60s* interview, op. cit.
[106] She kept pronouncing *papyri* this way in her lecture at a pastors' conference, sold by her as Riplinger *Testimony, Q & A*.
[107] She kept pronouncing *papyri* this way throughout the Temple Baptist Church lecture, op. cit.
[108] Berean Baptist Church lecture, op. cit.

	is no *Sumerian Pentateuch*.]
Shepherd of Hermas (*her mahs*)	Shepherd of Her-meez [109]
sophronizo (*sober* in Greek, Titus 2:4)	so-bron and so-pron [110]
Deisidaimonesteros (*dee cee dahee mon es ter oss*) [Greek]	dye-see-dye-moan-us-terrus [111]
Ugaritic (*yoo gah' rit ick*)	Yoo-gartick [112] [She also spelled it as Ugartic, several times in *New Age Bible Versions*, until correcting it in later printings.]
Verdant (*'vur dnt*)	Vare-dunt and vur-delt [113] [It is puzzling why she added an *L* sound to the end of *verdant*. *Verdant* comes from Latin, a language with which Gail has expressed familiarity]
discernment (*di' sern ment*)	dee-sern-ment [114]
The Correct Word with Correct Pronunciation	**How Riplinger Mispronounces the Word**
discerned (*di' serned*)	dee-cerned [115]

---

[109] *Transparent Translations*, Prophecy Club lecture, sold by Riplinger's A.V. Publications, Corp.
[110] Temple Baptist Church lectures, op. cit., Sunday school lecture.
[111] WBLW Radio interview on "Rise and Shine Time," 11/19/2009, op. cit.
[112] She continually pronounced it this way in the Prophecy Club lecture, op. cit.
[113] Temple Baptist Church lecture and *Action 60s* Interview, op. cit.
[114] Temple Baptist Church lecture, op. cit.

Theopneustos (*thay op' noo stoss*) [Greek word "God-inspired" or "inspired of God."]	theo-noo-stoss [116]
pedophile (*'ped ah file*)	peedah-file [117]
lineage (*'linee ij*)	lin-ij [118]
eschew (*es' ch oo*)	eh-choo [119]
Tarot (*'tare oh*)	terret [120]
Concupiscence (*con 'kyoopi sense*; *cun 'kyoopi sense*)	Con kyoop 'essence [121]
Ben Chayyim (*Ḥayyīm*) [Hebrew text]	[Ben] high-keem [122]
Ben Shachar (*shah har*) [Isa 14:12]	[Ben] Shuh-kar [123]
Jeconiah [son of OT king Jehoiakim, spelled Jechonias in the NT]	Jackah-nye-us [124]
kokab (*koh kawb*) [*star* in	koh-cab [125]

---

[115] *Action 60s* interview, op. cit.
[116] She does not pronounce the *P*.
[117] WBLW Radio interview, "Rise and Shine Time," 11/19/2009, op. cit.
[118] Berean Baptist Church lecture (2nd visit); Temple Baptist (multiple times).
[119] WBLW Radio interview, 11/19/2009. "Rise and Shine Time," op. cit.
[120] *Action 60s* interview, op. cit.
[121] Temple Baptist Church lectures, op. cit.
[122] Ibid.
[123] Ibid.
[124] She repeatedly mispronounces Jeconiah (Jechonias) as Jackah-nye-us in her Berean Baptist Church lecture (2nd visit) and in her Prophecy Club lecture.

Hebrew]	
Mobius (*moo' bee us*)	mow-bee-us [126]
helel [*hay layl*]	hil-lell [127]
shoal (*shole*)	show-el [128]
tomoye, tomoe	tim-oh-tee [129] [There is no second *T* sound]
emerods [*emmer ods*]	emmer-roids [130] [She also spelled it this way on the overhead transparency, even though it is spelled *emerods* in the KJV]
Collocation (*kahlah kay shun*) [a linguistics term]	co-location [131] [Despite the double *L*s indicating a short O sound in the first syllable, Riplinger pronounced it with a long O]
obelus (singular, *ah buh las*), obeli (plural, *ah buh lye*)	oh-bel-iss and oh-bel-ists [132]
Marcion	Mar-cone [133]

---

[125] Berean Baptist Church lectures, second visit, op. cit., and Temple Baptist Saturday night lecture, op. cit.
[126] Temple Baptist Church lectures and Prophecy Club lecture.
[127] She repeatedly mispronounces this in her Berean Baptist Church (2nd visit) lecture.
[128] Temple Baptist lectures.
[129] *Transparent Translations*, Prophecy Club lecture.
[130] Berean Baptist Church (2nd visit) lecture, op. cit.
[131] Berean Baptist lecture (2nd visit).
[132] *Transparent Translations*, Prophecy Club lecture.

WHO IS GAIL RIPLINGER? | 137

Pythagoras (*Pi' thag ah rus*)	Pythagah-reeus [134]
The Correct Word with Correct Pronunciation	**How Riplinger Mispronounces the Word**
Pantaenus (*pan tay ah nes*)	Pan-tah-nay-us [135]
Ulfilas/Wulfila	Oof-uh-liss [136]
Pamphilus (*pam feel us*)	Pam-phil-eeus [137]
[St. John] Chrysostom ('*Kris uh stum*; *Kris' ah stum*)	Krissah-zohme [138]
[Zane] Hodges and [Arthur] Farstad [These two men put together the Majority Text underlying the NKJV]	Hardge and Farnsted; [139] Hodge and Farnsted [140]
[Burton L.] Goddard (*god-dard*)	Good-erd, [141] Good-er [142]
[Newt] Gingrich (*ging-rich*)	Ghin-rick [143]

---

[133] She continually pronounces his name this way in every interview and lecture I have heard her give, e.g., Temple Baptist Church, Southwest Radio Church interviews, Riplinger Testimony Q & A, et. al.
[134] Temple Baptist lectures, op. cit.
[135] Berean Baptist Church lecture (1st visit), op. cit.
[136] *Transparent Translators*, Prophecy Club lecture.
[137] She frequently pronounces his name this wa in the Temple Baptist lectures, op. cit.
[138] Ibid.
[139] Ibid, plus other lectures.
[140] She repeatedly calls these two men this throughout her Q & A session of *Riplinger Testimony and Q & A*.
[141] She pronounced his name this way during a lecture at Berean Baptist Church (2nd visit), op. cit. Temple Baptist Church Sunday school lecture, op. cit.
[142] *Transparent Translations*, Prophecy Club lecture.

Precurse: (a *noun*, obsolete) "something that presages a future event."[144]	She used this word as a verb when it has no verb form: "But this was **precursed** by Madame Blavatsky…"[145] [No such word exists, even in *Webster's Third New International Dictionary, Unabridged. Precurse* occurs only as a noun: person, place, or thing.]

A person does not need to be a linguistics expert to find such mispronunciations grating to the ears. A linguistics expert is at least able to sound out words correctly. If Mrs. Riplinger did not proclaim herself a "linguistics expert," it would be simpler to go easy on her about her word mispronunciations. But if a person is going to declare herself an expert in an area in which she clearly demonstrates she is not, then for the sake of truth it must be addressed.

Regarding the word *verdant* (above, in the chart), Riplinger said she has no idea what it means and had never seen it before reading it in the NKJV. A true linguistics expert is going to know this word in the very least of their knowledge, and if by some stretch they really have never heard of it, they are going to look it up in a dictionary. *Verdant* simply means "green with grass or other rich vegetation; of the bright green color of lush grass."[146] It came into English via French from Latin. Personally, I learned what this word meant when I was in the eleventh grade. I saw it in a *National Geographic* article about Ireland, where it was used to describe the rich, green landscape. I looked it up in a dictionary and learned what it meant, and never forgot it. And I am no linguistics expert.

---

[143] Ibid.
[144] *Webster's Third New International Dictionary*, Unabridged, op. cit.
[145] *Transparent Translations*, Prophecy Club lecture.
[146] *New Oxford American Dictionary*.

Concerning Riplinger's mispronunciation of Burton L. Goddard's last name ["Goodard"], one does not need to be a "linguistics expert" to know that an *O* followed by double *D*'s does not make the same sound that double *O*'s do, which often rhyme with the word *good*. His name is pronounced GODdard, not GOODard. And how did Riplinger get "Hardge" from *Hodges* and "Farnsted" from *Farstad*? In *New Age Bible Versions*, she spells Hodges' name several times as "Hodge." [147]

Is it *Copyrighted* or *Copywritten*? *Proofread* or *Proofwritten*?

On several occasions, Riplinger has erroneously referred to works that are or are not *copyrighted* as "copywritten":

> **The King James Bible is not copywritten.** ... But, on the new versions, they **are copywritten**. ... Now, the copyright law under which **the new versions are copywritten** is called the "derivative copyright law." [148]

> ...all of **the new versions are copywritten** and the copyright law says... [149]

The inside cover of the fourth through 14th printings of *New Age Bible Versions* state:

---

[147] *New Age Bible Versions*, pp. 454, 477. On p. 454: "Zane C. Hodge." On p. 477, she quotes from D.A. Carson's book *The King James Version Debate* (p. 49) as "Hodge contends that because most of the early manuscripts..." In his book, Carson correctly spells Hodges' name. As of the 14th printing of Riplinger's book, these errors have not been corrected.
[148] Berean Baptist Church lectures (1st visit), op. cit. Lecture series sold by Riplinger's A.V. Publications, Corp.
[149] Transparent Translations, Prophecy Club lecture.

> Note to the reader: ... 2) The NIV and NASB do not have identical wording because **each is copywritten**. [Emphasis added]

Instead of saying they are *copyrighted*, she says they are "copywritten." Riplinger's use of the word does not exist in the English language. There is *copyright* and *copyrighted*. A *copyright* is "the exclusive legal right given to an originator or an assignee to print, publish, perform, film, or record literary, artistic, or musical material, and to authorize others to do the same."[150] The word is not in *Webster's Unabridged Third New International Dictionary*. When something has a copyright, it is *copyrighted*. Of *copywritten*, the Wiktionary states: "Common misconstruction of copyrighted."[151] *Copywriting* is "the text of advertisements or publicity material."[152]

In her loquacious assault on James White, Riplinger confirms "The NIV and NASB do not have identical words **because each is copywritten**" and that this "notice appears on the copyright page of almost every copy of New Age Bible Versions in print [and we have confirmed this as true]."[153] Likewise, in her rant on David Cloud, she said: "Cloud seems unaware that since both **the NIV and NASB are both copywritten**, they cannot legally use the same words."[154] The NIV and NASB are "copywritten"? When a *copywriter* writes public material, it has nothing to do with being *copyrighted*. However, when an author obtains a *copyright*, his/her work becomes *copyrighted*. We suspect that Mr. Cloud is aware of the difference.

Unfortunately, some who repeat quotes from Riplinger's books on the Internet have followed Riplinger's lead, using the word

---

[150] The *New Oxford American Dictionary*.
[151] http://en.wiktionary.org/wiki/copywritten. During an Internet search, we found dozens of people incorrectly using copywritten in place of copyrighted.
[152] The *New Oxford American Dictionary*.
[153] G.A. *Riplinger's Response to James White's Criticism of New Age Bible Versions: The James White Controversy* – Part 6. On line at Riplinger's web page: http://www.avpublications.com/avnew/content/Critiqued/james6.html.
[154] Riplinger's *O Madmen*, Part Two, can be read at her web page: http://www.avpublications.com/5_critiques/o_mm_pt2.htm.

"copywritten" instead of *copyrighted*. It is rather astounding that Riplinger has not corrected her error, after all these years.

During her question and answer session at a pastors' conference, Riplinger stated:

> Now, **the first edition of the book was never proofwritten**, I was too ill to do it. The pastor of the church that I was going to at the time said, "Get it out, get it out," and I was too ill **and it went out un-proofwritten.** [155]

As with "copywritten," there is no such word as "proofwritten" or "un-proofwritten." The correct word is *proofread*: (verb) "read (printer's proofs or other written or printed material) and mark any errors."[156] Just how often does Riplinger consult a dictionary? One may wonder how long she kept her job of teaching English to foreigners.

False Impressions

Riplinger has presented a different portrait of herself than what the facts show. As some are apt to say, "Things that are different are not the same." So, the questions for Riplinger remain: What is the real story and why has she not told the truth? Is she uncomfortable with who she is? Why is there the need to exaggerate and appear more successful than she is? God calls it lying.

To Noah Hutchings, Riplinger said:

> **Academic credentials have never been God's criteria for using a person.** Moses did not go to Desert State for forty years. God warns us in Psalm 62:9, "men of high degree are a lie." [157]

---

[155] *Riplinger Testimony and Q & A*, sold by Riplinger's A.V. Publications, Corp.
[156] The *New Oxford English Dictionary*.
[157] *Which Bible is God's Word?*, op. cit., p. 6.

It is mystifying why Riplinger has exaggerated her credentials, making them appear greater than they actually are, if she truly believes what she said. Contrary to her words, Psalm 62:9 is *not* about university degrees but about people born into either low or high status in life and how they both come to the same end. Once again, Riplinger tosses aside the context of the scripture for her own use. When will the pastors who defend her, who are supposed to *know* God's word, going to correct her and ask her to stop?

During the KNIS Radio interview, Riplinger said:

> We know a Proverb that says—Proverbs 10:31—"The froward tongue shall be cut out." *Froward* means *lying*, of course. ... **[I]t's within the power of each of us, every day, to repent.**

It should be in Riplinger's best interest to heed her own words, before it becomes too late. We can only hope that she will not choose to bitterly retaliate the truth being told. Whenever she does decide to genuinely repent, the public will know it because it is the public she has wronged and to whom she owes a public apology. Only those who truly repent love the truth and are able to honestly apologize. Those who repent will forsake their lying ways and it will be evident to all.

INDEX

1 Corinthians 14
    34, 11, 14, 20, 21, 61
1 Corinthians 7
    10-11, 39, 35
    13, 40
    39, 35, 36
1 John 1
    6, 65
    8, 10, 64
1 John 2
    3-4, 64
1 Timothy 2
    12, 10, 11
1 Timothy 4
    12, 57
1990s, 5, 14, 17, 18, 19, 20, 22, 36, 45, 55, 71, 75, 88, 89, 100
2 Peter 3
    11, 58
2 Samuel 20
    16, 6, 9
A.V. Publications, Corp., 17, 22, 23, 37, 50, 52, 53, 70, 71, 72, 73, 76, 77, 88, 95, 97, 100, 101, 104, 134, 139, 141
abandonment, 29, 32
Abimelech, 6, 7, 8
academic credentials, 26, 96, 116
adultery, 25, 29, 32, 33, 35, 36, 43, 44, 45, 46, 47, 54, 55, 59, 66
Architecture, 104, 105, 106, 107, 108, 109, 110, 111, 112
Bachelor of Arts, 103
bedridden, 73, 75, 78, 79, 84, 91, 93
Benny Hinn, 19
Berean Baptist Church, 11, 17, 24, 71, 75, 76, 114, 133, 135, 136, 137, 139
Bereans, 13
Bible Answer Man, 96
Bibliotheca Bodmeriana, 75
Bryn Riplinger Shutt, 16, 27, 33
Chester Beatty Library, 75
citizen ambassador program, 129
Colossians 3
    18, 35, 61
Complaint for Divorce, 28, 29, 32, 34
contradictions, 70, 71, 79, 80, 85, 87, 90, 93, 94
copywritten, 139, 140, 141
Cornell University, 113
court record, 45
Deborah, 5, 6, 7, 10, 12, 13, 60, 61
Dewayne Sands, 16, 27
disability, 73, 74, 75, 76, 77, 78, 79, 84, 86, 87, 88, 89, 90, 93, 94, 116
Dr. H. Wayne House, 125
Dr. James Sightler, 48
Eastern mysticism, 39

Ephesians 5
  22, 35, 61
  24, 35
false accusation, 34
First Baptist Church of
  Hammond, Indiana, 114
Gail Kaleda, 30, 31, 32, 41, 46,
  50, 97, 101, 120
Gail Latessa, 28
Gail Ludwig, 32, 34, 40, 50,
  54, 83, 102, 103, 118
Gospel Light Baptist Church,
  22, 24, 77, 78, 89, 115
Greek, 6, 45, 88, 122, 123, 124,
  125, 126, 133, 134, 135
Hazardous Materials, 20
helel, 136
Home Economics, 30, 50, 99,
  103, 105, 106, 107, 108,
  109, 111, 113, 115, 116, 117
homosexuality, 26, 28, 32, 33,
  34
Honor Society, 126, 127, 128
honorary doctorate, 114
Hyles-Anderson College, 16,
  27, 114
hypocrisy, 58, 59
In Awe of Thy Word, 97, 101,
  102, 110, 112, 113, 119, 128
Interior Design, 30, 50, 72, 82,
  84, 99, 100, 102, 103, 104,
  105, 106, 107, 108, 109,
  110, 111, 112, 116
Jack Hyles, 114
Jael, 5, 6, 7, 10, 12, 13, 60, 61
Jim Baker., 19
Joab, 6, 7, 9

John 3
  19-21, 22
John Rylands Library, 75
Judges 17
  6, 7, 8
Kaleda, 18, 30, 31, 32, 33, 34,
  37, 38, 39, 40, 41, 43, 44,
  45, 47, 50, 51, 53, 54, 55,
  102, 103, 118
Kent State University, 17, 23,
  24, 26, 30, 31, 34, 39, 42,
  50, 54, 71, 74, 75, 79, 84,
  87, 88, 91, 92, 93, 96, 98,
  99, 100, 101, 102, 103, 104,
  105, 107, 108, 109, 111,
  112, 113, 114, 115, 116,
  117, 118
KJV Ditches Blind Guides, 56
Landmark Anchor, 16, 93
Latessa, 18, 28, 29, 32, 33, 37,
  55, 102
legal separation, 18
Leonard Sweet, 19
linguist, 132, 133
linguistics, 132, 133, 136, 138,
  139
linguistics expert, 132, 133,
  138, 139
living epistles, 21
lying, 14, 22, 37, 40, 45, 46,
  49, 57, 59, 62, 63, 65, 66,
  67, 69, 70, 95, 96, 112, 141,
  142
Mahoning County Court of
  Common Pleas, 29
Mark 10
  12, 35, 45

marriage record, 33
martyr complex, 93
Mary Magdalene, 5, 6, 11
Master of Arts, 103
Master of Fine Arts, 50, 103
Matthew 19
  5-6, 35
Matthew 5
  32, 47
Michael Riplinger, 41, 42, 43, 44, 47, 49, 50, 52, 67, 106
Mickey Carter, 16, 69, 93
Mortar Board Honor Societ, 127
New Age Bible Versions, 12, 13, 14, 18, 26, 27, 31, 67, 74, 75, 76, 79, 84, 86, 87, 88, 89, 94, 95, 97, 99, 101, 102, 114, 117, 119, 125, 128, 134, 139, 140
New Age bookstore, 74, 75, 86, 91, 92
Niles, Ohio, 18, 28, 29, 37
Nite Line video interview, 95
Noah Hutchings, 74, 77, 96, 98, 115, 126, 127, 141
Paula White, 19
People to People International, 129, 130, 131
Peter Popoff, 19
Phil Kidd, 12
physical anomaly, 26, 28, 33
placenta previa, 83, 84
Portage County, Ohio, 30, 31, 51
post-graduate study, 99
Prentice Hall, 101

professor, 6, 23, 24, 52, 54, 74, 75, 97, 100, 102, 109, 114, 115, 116, 117, 125, 126
proofwritten, 141
Proverbs 30
  20, 24
Proverbs 6
  26-29, 47
  35, 44
Proverbs 7, 47
public teacher, 15
Pythagoras, 137
question-and-answer sessions, 11
research, 14, 72, 74, 75, 76, 78, 79, 81, 84, 86, 87, 89, 91, 92, 93, 97, 99, 105, 113, 117, 118, 122, 128
Rick Warren, 19
Rob Bell, 19
Robert Tilton, 19
Roman Catholic, 18, 19, 26, 37, 72
Romans 1
  32, 19, 57
Romans 7
  2a-3, 36
  3, 46
second marriage, 26, 30, 34
Separation Agreement, 28, 29, 32, 34, 40, 50, 54
Sheba, 7, 9
Shepherd of Hermas, 134
Sisera, 6, 7
soap operas, 56
Southwest Radio Church, 77, 126, 137

Sri Aurobindo, 39
teaching men, 9
Ted Haggard, 19
Temple Baptist Church, 7, 11, 17, 23, 37, 71, 76, 100, 115, 133, 134, 135, 136, 137
terminal degree, 50, 103, 104, 105, 106, 107, 116, 117
textbooks, 26, 97, 98, 99, 100, 101, 102, 108, 112, 117, 118
The Language of the King James Bible, 78, 97, 102, 119
The Prophecy Club, 109
The Shining Ones, 38
the wise woman of 2 Samuel, 5
the wise woman of Abel, 9, 10
the woman in the tower, 8
Theopneustos, 135
third marriage, 57
Traitors, 55, 70
Transcendental Meditation, 38, 39
Truth and Life, 30, 31
Which Bible is God's Word?, 5, 74, 77, 96, 98, 102, 109, 115, 119, 126, 127, 129, 141
willful dishonesty, 69
willful sin, 19, 57, 62, 64
woman at the well, 22
Youngstown, Ohio, 28

www.ingramcontent.com/pod-product-compliance
Lightning Source LLC
Chambersburg PA
CBHW051714090426
42736CB00013B/2703